Praise for *Amer*...

As John Fanestil expertly demonstrates in *American Heresy*, the idea that the United States occupies a special place in the divine economy extends back to the colonial era, and the nation's founders drew on English Protestant notions of divine protection and providence. White Christian nationalism, he argues, traffics in "violence, nostalgia, racism, propaganda, conspiratorial thinking, and nationalism," and we ignore the religious reverberations of America's past at our peril. Self-examination and repentance are in order, even for those who identify as Christian progressives. This is a thoughtful, provocative, and well-argued book.

—Dr. Randall Balmer, John Phillips Chair in Religion at Dartmouth College and author of *Saving Faith: How American Christianity Can Reclaim Its Prophetic Voice*

This book deserves a place on the shelf among the expanding set of works exploring the origins and dangers of white Christian nationalism. Conservatives and progressives alike would benefit from the book—and find it challenging some of their presuppositions about politics today and the founding of the United States. We need authors like John Fanestil who help us see beyond the near-sightedness of our present moment.

—Rev. Dr. Brian Kaylor, president and editor-in-chief of *Word & Way* and author of *Presidential Campaign Rhetoric in an Age of Confessional Politics*

This is a book that will make those of us who are white, Christian, and American uncomfortable, but it's a necessary discomfort that comes from examining the complexity of the past. John Fanestil has marshaled impressive historical evidence to show that Christian heresy and Christian truth were more deeply intertwined in the thinking of the American founders than we might have assumed, and that American Christians today—whether conservative or progressive—are more strongly affected by this legacy than most of us realize.

—Dr. Daniel K. Williams, professor of history at the University of West Georgia and author of *The Politics of the Cross: A Christian Alternative to Partisanship*

AMERICAN HERESY

AMERICAN HERESY

The Roots and Reach of White Christian Nationalism

JOHN FANESTIL

Fortress Press
Minneapolis

AMERICAN HERESY
The Roots and Reach of White Christian Nationalism

Library of Congress Control Number: 2023007387 (print)

Cover design and illustration: Brice Hemmer

Print ISBN: 978-1-5064-8923-0
eBook ISBN: 978-1-5064-8924-7

To Jennifer, again

Contents

Deep Roots

More and more Americans are taking stock of white racism in America. The Black Lives Matter movement has dramatized the continuing victimization of Black Americans at the hands of law enforcement, and efforts like Bryan Stevenson's The Innocence Project have highlighted the deep injustice of our nation's long-standing practice of mass incarceration. Historians like Ibram X. Kendi (*Stamped from the Beginning*) and journalists like Nikole Hannah-Jones (*The 1619 Project*) have placed white racism and the violence of slavery, Jim Crow, segregation, and institutionalized discrimination at the center of the telling of American history, alongside the long struggle of African American resistance to these injustices. Talk of reparations for the descendants of enslaved Americans continues to spread, as do endeavors to "decolonize" the American public square, ranging from dismantling Confederate monuments to the repatriation of Indigenous artifacts from our nation's museums. Attempts to address the complexities of race and the realities of racism in American public schools continue to multiply, even as they provoke fierce opposition from those who decry what they call "critical race theory."[1]

The current moment is one of special reckoning for Americans who are—as I am—both white and Christian, for in recent years the deep connection between white racism and American Christianity has been put on prominent public display. Why did Donald Trump choose to pose in front of a church, holding a Bible, as law enforcement officers dressed in riot gear forcibly cleared Lafayette Square near the White House during the George Floyd protests on June 1, 2020? And why were so many people carrying not just American flags but also religious-themed banners, Bibles, and other totems of the Christian religion as they stormed the US Capitol on January 6, 2021? Why have the rituals of Christian worship become staples of right-wing political rallies, and why do white supremacists like the Proud Boys begin their gatherings with Christian prayer?[2]

"What are they thinking?" I have found myself muttering more than once these last few years. Perhaps you have found yourself muttering this question, too.

How has this toxic mix of white racism, conspiratorial thinking, hyper-masculinity, and rabid nationalism flourished in a religious tradition birthed from breaking down the dividing lines of nation, class, and gender? The Apostle Paul wrote to the early Christian community in Galatia that in Christ Jesus "there is neither Jew nor Greek, male nor female, slave nor free" (Galatians 3:28). Yet millions of white American Christians have been pleased to join their voices to the rallying cry, "America First." And how has political violence flourished in a tradition founded by a man who preached and practiced nonviolence? All four of the New Testament gospels tell the story of Jesus denouncing the disciple (John's gospel says it was Simon Peter) who drew his sword to strike the soldier charged with executing Jesus's arrest (John 18:15–18). Yet some white Americans today are pleased to pose with assault rifles for the photos they mail to friends at Christmastime.[3] How did expressions of faith like these become entrenched in American Christianity? What can account for their staying power in American society?

Understanding an ideology called "white Christian nationalism" can help us answer these questions. Philip Gorski and

Samuel Perry have defined white Christian nationalism as "a deep story" that functions "like a bare-bones movie script" in shaping popular understandings. They outline the story this way:

> America was founded as a Christian nation by (white) men who were "traditional" Christians, who based the nation's founding documents on "Christian principles." The United States is blessed by God, which is why it has been so successful; and the nation has a special role to play in God's plan for humanity. But these blessings are threatened by cultural degradation from "un-American" influences both inside and outside our borders.

According to Gorski and Perry, adherents of white Christian nationalism believe "America has been entrusted with a sacred mission: to spread religion, freedom, and civilization—by force, if necessary."[4]

But white Christian nationalism is not a fringe movement embraced only by a violent few. It is not something that exists "out there," in a group of "others." Polling by Perry and others shows that the attitudes associated with white Christian nationalism thrive along a spectrum and can be found within every Christian denomination. If those of us who are white and American and Christian are honest with ourselves, we will recognize ourselves on this spectrum. White Christian nationalism is a spiritual inheritance shared by all white American Christians, not just those who march in white supremacist demonstrations or who stormed the US Capitol building on January 6, 2021.[5]

To understand white Christian nationalism in this broader sense, we must recognize it as a religious movement with deep roots in American history. We must confront the truth that dramatic displays of white resentment, radicalism, and racism like those we have witnessed in recent years reflect deep convictions that are neither marginal nor novel to American culture. Rather, they reflect a brand of Christian religiosity that is intrinsically American. This religiosity can be traced to the very earliest English colonization of North America. It played a critical—in this book I will argue indispensable—role in the founding of the United States. It has never ceased from shaping the spiritual lives of white Americans and our nation's public landscape.

In this book I will uncover the deep roots of white Christian nationalism, its role in the founding of the United States, and its continuing powerful reach in contemporary American life.

A Christian Nation?

Was the United States of America founded as a Christian nation? This question dominates public conversation about the role played by religion in American life. The question frames the debate in an either/or way, inviting a "yes" or "no" answer, and fracturing the conversation along ideological lines.

As a rule, liberals and progressives resist the notion that religion played an important, much less decisive, role in the American founding. American progressives today celebrate the secular strains of American origins—the rising tide of Enlightenment thought and modern science, the constitution of a nonsectarian republic, the separation of church and state. They like to think of the American revolutionaries as living at the cutting edge of intellectual developments in the late eighteenth century, and they embrace those Founding Fathers who openly expressed suspicion of religious traditions and motivations—think Benjamin Franklin or Thomas Jefferson. Progressives see the high-minded ideals expressed in foundational documents like the Declaration of Independence and the US Constitution as moving *beyond* what they think of as the restrictive religious worldview of colonial America. The vision of American nationhood implicit in this claim is that

the religious character of early American life is not representative of the real America, the "true America," the America that
America was meant to become.* In the view of the most strident secular progressives—the comedian Bill Maher comes to
mind—to be religious is to be a dupe and runs counter to the
American spirit, which is liberal and enlightened. Progressives
take encouragement from polls showing continued declines
in religious affiliation among younger generation Americans.
For the United States to become "a more perfect union," the
religious character of American life must be overcome or tran-
scended, someday to vanish from the public square.

Conservative Americans, meanwhile, are more likely to
embrace what they see as the religious roots of the American
experiment. The English and other Europeans who colonized
North America were overwhelmingly Christian, and so too
were the men who wrote the Declaration of Independence and
the US Constitution. Many of the founders—Samuel Adams
and Patrick Henry are favorites—were enthusiastic defenders
of the Christian faith, and even "enlightened" founders like
Jefferson remained devoted to the religious institutions and
values that shaped their lives. Conservatives see the motivations and aims of the founders as shaped indelibly by their religious convictions—thus America was founded as "a Christian
nation"—and many understand this to have been the result of
God's providential design. Adherents of this worldview—think
Mike Huckabee or Mike Pence—believe that "true Americans"
are those who embrace "traditional Christianity" or at

---

* In this book I will sometimes use "America" as a shorthand for the
  United States and "Americans" as a shorthand for citizens and/or
  residents of the United States. I recognize that citizens and residents
  of many other countries in "the Americas" find this prevailing vernacular in the United States presumptuous. In a like fashion, I will
  sometimes use the terms "Indians" and "Native Americans" as a
  shorthand for the Indigenous peoples of North America, conforming to the current (and imprecise) usage.

minimum champion the view that moral claims rooted in the "Judeo-Christian tradition" are fundamental to the health of the American body politic. Conservative religious Americans see indicators of religion's decline as warning signs, not harbingers of hope. Movements of moral renewal and spiritual revival are needed to restore American greatness, and so these movements are to be fervently hoped for, prayed for, and worked for.

But what if the debate inspired by this contemporary ideological divide causes us to miss something essential about religion in early America? What if a particular brand of Christian religiosity indeed played a decisive role in the American founding? But what if this same religiosity tempted its adherents to embrace heretical expressions of the Christian faith?

In his 1922 book, *What I Saw in America*, the Englishman G. K. Chesterton famously characterized America as "a nation with the soul of a church." What if the church that is the soul of America is—and always has been—"sin-sick" with white Christian nationalism?

In *American Heresy* I will argue that we cannot understand the current moment in American public life without understanding how a distinctly American brand of Protestant religiosity shaped the lives of America's revolutionary generations. This religiosity inspired the English who colonized North America—including the Founding Fathers of the United States—to embrace noble values like order, destiny, progress, innovation, independence, and patriotism. But this religiosity also tempted the people who first called themselves Americans to embrace practices of violence, nostalgia, racism, propaganda, conspiracy, and nationalism. These are the bitter fruits of white Christian nationalism, a pernicious and distinctly American strain of Christian thought and practice that is, at present, in a season of renewed flowering. In this way of thinking, the Christian religion played a critical role in the founding of the United States, but the brand of Christianity that played this critical role was in important ways a Christian heresy.[6]

The word *heresy* can be defined most simply as "false teaching," but scholars of religion are quick to emphasize that one person's heresy is another's orthodoxy. Who decides which is which?

I consider white Christian nationalism a Christian heresy because it encourages adherents to celebrate the English colonization of North America as a divine calling superior to God's calling on other peoples. It presumes divine sanction for the enterprise of American nation-building, and it makes an idol of the United States as the first among nations in the eyes of God— the "greatest nation on earth." In this it violates the first great commandment of the Hebrew Bible: "I am the LORD your God, who brought you out of the land of Egypt, out of the house of slavery. You shall have no other gods before Me" (Deuteronomy 5:6–7). Jesus affirmed the essential challenge of the spiritual life to be twofold—to "Love the Lord your God with all your heart and with all your soul and with all your strength and with all your mind" and to "Love your neighbor as yourself" (Matthew 22:36–40). When we as Americans succumb to the temptations of white Christian nationalism, we embrace impoverished forms of Christian thought and practice that fail to meet this essential challenge.

The notion that the American founding was rooted deeply in heretical expressions of the Christian faith challenges us to consider the United States as kin to other nations founded on ideologies of white-settler colonialism, nations like Rhodesia and South Africa, Australia, and New Zealand. The sociologist Pierre van den Berghe has called these "Herrenvolk" societies, using the German phrase for "master race" (literally, "the Lord's People"). In a Herrenvolk society, a certain race or caste of people take for granted that they and their kinfolk occupy a place of divinely sanctioned privilege. Leaders of Herrenvolk societies perpetuate sustained and rigid forms of inequality while espousing egalitarian and democratic values. A Herrenvolk democracy, according to van den Berghe, is "democratic for the master race but tyrannical for subordinate groups."[7] Of the American founding he concludes simply: "The democratic, egalitarian, and libertarian ideals were reconciled with slavery and genocide by restricting the definition of humanity to whites." Americans are accustomed to thinking of apartheid South Africa in these stark terms, but few white Americans have ever considered our own national origins in this way.

Is it right to understand that the United States was founded on Herrenvolk principles? Even to ask the questions invites a frank consideration of American history and leads to a few simple, inescapable observations:

- The genocide and mass dislocation of Native peoples, and the mass enslavement and torture of African captives and their descendants, were indispensable to our nation's founding.
- The project of nation-building required the sustained exercise of extraordinary, institutionalized violence and the indiscriminate—usually lawless—seizing of land.
- The early American elites who oversaw this project were overwhelmingly white and male and Protestant, and they took for granted that these characteristics were emblematic of what it meant to be both "Christian" and "American."
- These elites believed the English colonization of North America, the success of the American Revolution, and the dramatic westward expansion of the new nation were not just justified but in fact divinely inspired.
- In championing these views, these white elites were supported by broad swaths of their white constituencies within the emerging democratic structures of the new republic. They were not outliers but were—as they are widely and rightly recognized today—"true Americans."

The views reflected in these assertions were, as we might say today, "features, not bugs" of the early American experiment. Together, these assertions represent a starting point for considering the deep roots and enduring reach of white Christian nationalism.

Framing the story of the American founding in this way presents a challenge to well-meaning white Americans of every religious and ideological disposition. First, it discourages white conservative Christians from romanticizing America's past. While it has seeded much that is good and noble about American culture, the passionate Protestantism that played an instrumental role in the American Revolution steeped our nation's founders—and continues to steep white Americans today—in passions and prejudices unbefitting followers of Jesus. Second, it discourages white progressive Christians from characterizing white Christian nationalism as a problem that exists only in "other kinds of Christians." This inheritance has helped shape every branch of American Christianity, and it continues to shape the spiritual lives of all white Christian Americans. And third, it challenges secular Americans from across the ideological spectrum to acknowledge that religion played a powerful role, for better and for worse, in the founding of the United States. To pretend that this was not so is to embrace a version of American origins that is as revisionist as is the romantic white Christian nationalist version that secular Americans rightly denounce. In short, *American Heresy* challenges all white Americans to acknowledge that white Christian nationalism is, and always has been, endemic to American culture.

Many white Americans like to say, when considering transparent expressions of white Christian nationalism, "that's not who we are." But as a historian who has studied American origins, and as a Christian pastor intimately familiar with the inner lives of white American Christians, I can tell you that this is an essential part of what it means to be white, American, and Christian.

Across three decades I have worked with many predominantly white churches from "mainline" Protestant denominations. People enthusiastically championing the ideals of white Christian nationalism have made themselves known to me in every congregation I have served. Most have done so forthrightly, unapologetically, simply assuming that I should accept the blending of white racism and American nationalism as a natural expression of the Christian faith. More tellingly, I have seen the powerful, subconscious influence of this heretical Christian thinking in the decision-making of well-meaning leaders at every level—from the chairs of missions committees to Sunday-school teachers. Last, but by no means least, I recognize and confess the influence of white Christian nationalism in my own life. Like all American children, I was introduced to the traditional story of American origins from the time that I was first taught to read. Throughout my life it has been easy and natural for me—a white American Protestant man—to embrace others who looked like me as the heroes of the story. I recognize and confess that I have often succumbed, in my personal and professional life, to the spiritual temptations that white Christian nationalism invites.

American Heresy invites all Americans to accept that our national history has been shaped by a pernicious strain of the Christian tradition that is rightly called white Christian nationalism. It extends a more intimate and personal challenge to those of us who consider ourselves white and Christian and American. It is easy to denounce extreme examples of white supremacy as perversions of the Christian faith. But we, too, are the descendants of white Christian nationalism, a distinctly American brand of Christian heresy.

Setting the Stage

This book is part of a larger project that is well underway, the project of reframing popular understandings of American history. Unlike many contributions to this project, this book does not seek to uncover the stories of people whose roles in the founding of the United States have been traditionally over-looked and undervalued. Others far better equipped than I am are pursuing this strategy, and many doing so have earned well-deserved platforms of prominence in the academy and in the public square.[8] This book, by contrast, places familiar characters at the center stage—Puritan colonists like John Winthrop, William Bradford, and Cotton Mather; Protestant preachers like Samuel Davies and George Whitefield; and leading revolu-tionaries like George Washington, Thomas Jefferson, Benjamin Franklin, Thomas Jefferson, Samuel Adams, and Patrick Henry. Rather than "decentering" these familiar characters—all white men—this book "recenters" them on the stage of white Christian nationalism.

Similarly, this book follows a very conventional narra-tive, tracing the roots of the American experiment from the early English colonization of New England, Virginia, and Pennsylvania to the forging of intercolonial bonds through the middle decades of the eighteenth century, culminating in the French and Indian War, the War of Independence, and the crafting of foundational documents in the Continental Congresses. Many today see this traditional narrative as masking the complexity of the early American experience. Indeed, the early English colonies in North America were shaped by different dynamics of conflict with diverse Native peoples, by varied encounters with explorers, wayfarers, traders, and colonizers from other European nations and by different flows of in-migration, including hundreds of thou-sands of Africans who were forcibly trafficked into the colo-nies through the transatlantic slave trade. English colonists in North America differed greatly, too, in matters of religious denomination, doctrine, and practice, and leaders of the colo-nies pursued different strategies of commercial, cultural, and political development, strategies that changed across time. Historians of early America are right to portray the story of American origins as much more complicated than the traditional narrative allows.

This book takes the traditional narrative of American beginnings and casts it in a new light. It does not presume to pass spiritual judgment on the American founders, nor to label them, individually, as Christian heretics. Instead, it shows how these familiar characters were shaped by—and helped give shape to—a distinctly American brand of Christian heresy, often succumbing to its temptations.

Each chapter of *American Heresy* follows the same, simple outline. Each begins by introducing how early English Protestants, broadly, understood a basic Christian doctrine— creation, providence, progress, salvation, liberty, and virtue. The first part of each chapter cites landmark primary sources to demonstrate how English Protestants grounded each concept in Scripture, which they understood to contain fundamental truths, including God's all-encompassing will for humankind. The beginnings of each chapter also emphasize the inherently dualistic and oppositional nature of the early English Protestant movement. Even as they bickered among themselves continually over the finer matters of doctrine and practice, early English Protestants agreed that the whole of human history had culminated in a battle between Christ and his "true Church," which promulgated the "good news" found in the scriptures, and the Roman Catholic Church, which they considered the chief agent of Satan on earth.

Each chapter next encapsulates how leaders of the English colonial enterprise appropriated these foundational Protestant understandings and adapted them to their new circumstances in North America. These new circumstances were characterized foundationally by conflict. English efforts to enlarge and demarcate their territorial boundaries in North America were routinely contested by their colonial competitors, the Catholic French and Spanish, and by the continent's many Native peoples. Over time English Protestants in North America came to think of the vast surrounding "wilderness" as occupied by "savage" Indians and "popish" French, whose frequent alliances seemed proof of a diabolical conspiracy. Developing a self-understanding as embattled and persecuted, the English colonists prosecuted near-perpetual war against the Native peoples of North America. They also fashioned and hardened a racialized system of "chattel" slavery. Along the way they began to distinguish themselves more sharply in racialized terms from their Indian foes and their African slaves—they began to think of themselves as "white." Across the colonies, this term became widely accepted as a proxy for an ethnic identity as people of English—or, sometimes, "Anglo-Saxon"—descent. They reframed the moniker "Christian," too, as a religious identity conjuring broad Protestant themes. One did not have to be English and Protestant to be considered white or Christian in the mid-eighteenth century, but white English Protestants in the colonies understood themselves to embody the normative definition of these terms.

Each chapter then describes how this spiritual inheritance shaped the men who would become leading figures in the American Revolution. Beginning in the mid-1750s, the English struggle for colonial supremacy in North America came to a head in what would come to be known in England as the "Seven Years' War," and in North America as the "French and Indian War." Leading English colonists failed to produce a formal union as they prosecuted this war, but they began to embrace a shared sense of "continental" destiny, and eventually the self-identification as "American." In the war's aftermath, they grew increasingly frustrated with Britain's postwar policies of taxation, trade, governance, and colonial expansion. Resistance to these policies provoked unprecedented levels of intercolonial collaboration in the buildup to the American Revolution. The revolutionaries forged a new kind of national solidarity in part by embracing republican political principles and democratic themes. But they also tapped ancient passions and suspicions among English Protestants who had been trained from childhood to believe that the exercise of Protestant ideals like "liberty" and "virtue" required perpetual vigilance and, frequently, armed insurrection.

Each chapter concludes by drawing connections between these foundational Protestant ways of thinking about the world, rooted deep in American history, and the things we are seeing played out in our public life today. These sections also include my personal reflections on what it means to be spiritually tempted by white Christian nationalism.

A Primer, Not a Panorama

As a "primer" on the origins of white Christian nationalism, this book does not attempt to provide a panorama spanning centuries. Instead, it offers a concise history of national origins with special emphasis on religious developments in British North America across the seventeenth and eighteenth centuries. In doing so, it draws specific connections between the founding of the United States and the kinds of things that may leave you scratching your head when you read them in your newspapers or your social media feeds today.

What are they thinking? If you have ever found yourself muttering this question while browsing the news, this book is for you. *American Heresy* answers this question by connecting the "deep roots" and the "long reach" of white Christian nationalism without detailing the length of every branch of the tree.

Throughout, this book makes one simple, straightforward argument: white Christian nationalism is a distinctly American brand of Christian heresy that has always been—and remains today—a driving force in American life.

Surely many who led the American Revolution and fought in the War of Independence did so in defense of hardscrabble economic interests, including control over the western lands that the colonists called "Indian Country." Surely many were deeply committed to political principles of representative government, famously summarized in the rallying cry "no taxation without representation." Surely many were inspired by the rising tide of Enlightenment ideals that Thomas Jefferson famously memorialized in the opening sentences of the Declaration of Independence. But most English colonists who fought in the American War of Independence also considered themselves the spiritual descendants of the "Glorious Revolution" by which William III and Mary II had restored the English monarchy to Protestant Rule in 1688, and of the English Bill of Rights, which William and Mary had signed into law the following year to enshrine the religious liberties that were explicitly associated with the Protestant cause. Many considered the revolutionary struggle entirely consistent with this cause, a cause for which their Protestant forebears had fought and died. Parsing out the multiple motivations of individual founders has tested the talents of generations of biographers, and ascribing priority and causality to these motivations in the aggregate has consumed the attention of generations of historians.

As much as the high-minded ideals that were written into the nation's founding documents, a distinctively American brand of passionate Protestant nationalism helped rally patriots to the revolutionary cause. Down through the ages, this spiritual inheritance has inspired Americans to embrace noble values like order, destiny, progress, innovation, independence, and patriotism. But this same inheritance renders especially white Americans perpetually susceptible to the temptations of white Christian nationalism: violence, nostalgia, racism, propaganda, conspiratorial thinking, and nationalism. These temptations are rooted deep in American history. They are the bitter fruits of an American heresy and are at present in a season of renewed flowering.

I am not alone in this way of thinking, and for this I am thankful. Scholars of religion across the nation continue to deepen our understanding of this cultural movement—Philip Gorksi at Yale, Samuel Perry at the University of Oklahoma, Andrew L. Whitehead at Indiana University-Purdue University Indianapolis (IUPUI), Kristin Kobes Du Mez at Calvin University, R. Marie Griffith at Washington University in St. Louis, Randall Balmer at Dartmouth College, Bradley Onishi at Skidmore College, and the independent scholar Jemar Tisby, to name just a few.[9] A network organizing against white Christian nationalism continues to grow, including through organizations like the Baptist Joint Committee for Religious Liberty; through leading public voices like Russell Moore (editor-in-chief at Christianity Today) and Robert P. Jones (founder of the Public Religion Research Institute); and through the work of journalists like Katherine Stewart, Tom LoBianco, and others. Thousands of religious leaders have signed the "Statement Against Christian Nationalism," declaring that "Christian nationalism seeks to merge Christian and American identities, distorting both the Christian faith and America's constitutional democracy." In endorsing this statement, Shane Claiborne has written:

> In ages past, we have seen distortions of the Christian faith that warrant a response. Church leaders have held emergency councils in order to unilaterally denounce mutations of orthodox faith, and to affirm the core values at the heart of Christianity. It is in that Spirit that we unite our diverse voices as Christian leaders to declare that "Christian" nationalism is a heresy.[10]

I have written this book in hopes of contributing to this unfolding conversation.

I am convinced that to resist the temptations of white Christian nationalism we must acknowledge the depth of its foothold in our national history. Only by understanding the true origins of this distinctly American heresy can we appreciate the full weight of this cultural inheritance. Only by understanding the ways of thinking and acting it inspires can we learn to work together to resist its enduring influence in our shared public life, and in ourselves.

CHAPTER 1

Creation
Order and Violence

For all their differences, most English colonists who migrated to North America before the American Revolution—and so, too, most of their American-born descendants—shared a common spiritual inheritance. They identified with the Protestant cause in the great English Civil Wars of the seventeenth century, a period of strife that was part of a larger, centuries-long conflict between popular Protestant movements across Europe and the prevailing authority of the Roman Catholic Church. This is a first key to understanding the deep roots of white Christian nationalism in America today: most of the English who first colonized North America in the seventeenth century—and most of their descendants, who came to call themselves "Americans" in the eighteenth century—were Protestants. Religiously speaking, they were birds of mostly common feather nested in different offshoots of a single branch of the Christian family tree.

As did their counterparts on the European continent, early English Protestants on both sides of the Atlantic believed that the Bible contained the authoritative account of how the world was brought into existence and the proper place of human beings in it. Early English Protestants brought to their reading of the Bible—as do all who read it—culturally conditioned assumptions, ways of thinking, and interpretive frameworks.

Among these were understandings about land and property that shaped the foundations of modern English and American jurisprudence, so powerfully, in fact, that most Americans still today would have trouble imagining that land and property could be understood in any other way.

The preference for order that characterizes so much of American life today can be traced to these ancient English understandings of the very nature of things. So, too, can the propensity to violence, which is a deep root of American white Christian nationalism.

The Doctrine of Creation

English Protestants understood that God had created all things from the very beginning of time. They also believed that God had made human beings responsible for bringing order to the created world. The King James Version of the Bible, first published in 1611, recounted the creation of the first man and woman this way:

> So God created man in his own image, in the image of God created he him; male and female he created them. And God blessed them, and God said unto them, Be fruitful and multiply, and replenish the earth, and subdue it: and have dominion over the fish of the sea, and over the fowl of the air, and over every living thing that moveth upon the earth. (Genesis 1:27–28, KJV)

As English Protestants understood it, this is precisely what it meant to have been created "in the image of God." Human beings were designed to exercise "dominion" over the natural world.

But early English Protestants also brought to this task of ordering creation their own ancient ways of thought and practice that were becoming more and more formalized as "English Common Law."[1] At its most fundamental level, the English understood that the human exercise of dominion required the "taming" of what they considered "wilderness." Wild lands could be tamed by "marking" them as common land ("the commons"), to which all members of the community had access, or by settling, enclosing, and cultivating them, at which point they became "private property," belonging to the rightful "owner." Any who abused the privileges of the commons were subject to sanction by the community—or even expulsion from it—and any who breached boundaries of private property were subject to punishment for "trespassing."

Devout English Protestants found warrant for these understandings in their sacred texts. In 1630, John Cotton preached a "farewell" sermon to a new company of pilgrims as they departed for the Massachusetts Bay colony. Born in 1584, Cotton was a precocious student, tutor, lecturer, and dean at Emmanuel College, Cambridge, which was well known as a "nursery of Puritanism." As a parish vicar in Boston, Lincolnshire, Cotton rebelled against Anglican customs in matters both liturgical and ecclesiastic, earning the esteem of John Winthrop and other members of the Massachusetts Bay Company. Entitled "God's Promise to His Plantation," Cotton's 1630 sermon was based on 2 Samuel 7:10: "Moreover I will appoint a place for my people Israel, and I will plant them, that they may dwell in a place of their owne, and move no more." From this Scripture, Cotton derived the simple conclusion that "The placing of a people in this or that Country is from the appointment of the Lord." He then proceeded to detail three ways in which "God makes room for a people" in a country which he has "espied" for them:

> First, when he casts out the enemies of a people before them by lawfull warre with the inhabitants, which God calls them unto: as in Ps. 44. 2. Thou didst drive out the Heathen before them. . . .
>   Secondly, when hee gives a forreigne people favour in the eyes of any native people to come and sit downe with them either by way of purchase, as Abraham did obtain the field of

Machpelah; or else when they give it in courtesie, as Pharoah did the land of Goshen unto the sons of Iacob.

Thirdly, when hee makes a Country though not altogether void of Inhabitants, yet void in that place where they reside. Where there is a vacant place, there is liberty for the sonnes of Adam or Noah to come and inhabite, though they neither buy it, nor aske their leaves.[2]

Cotton's sermon amounted to a theological defense of English colonization, casting the New England colonists in the role of the people of Israel, whose journey from captivity in Egypt to the "promised land" of Canaan is chronicled in the biblical narrative of the Exodus. In 1633 Cotton fled England for Massachusetts, where he joined the pastoral team at the First Church of Boston and produced a family that would include his namesake grandson, the famous Puritan preacher Cotton Mather.

English Protestants influenced by Enlightenment thought arrived at much these same conclusions while convincing themselves that they did so through the application of pure reason. Students of American history commonly associate this way of thinking with John Locke, whose writings would become so popular among leading American colonists in the mid-eighteenth century that his name functioned almost as a ritual incantation in revolutionary circles.[3] Locke is rightly characterized as a luminary of the English Enlightenment, but his philosophizing was as much an extension of his English Protestant upbringing as it was a departure from it. Born in 1632 to a Puritan family near Bristol, Locke was educated at Christ Church, Oxford, where he embraced new schools of thought in philosophy and medicine. During a five-year exile in Amsterdam, he immersed himself both in the English community of dissenting Protestants and in the city's free-thinking culture. Locke returned to England in 1688, after the English Crown and church were returned to Protestant rule under William III and Mary II. This so-called Glorious Revolution reestablished the free exercises of speech and publication on which both dissenting Protestants and "free thinkers" depended. In this atmosphere Locke became a leading champion of the "natural law tradition." As Justin Dyer has neatly summarized, this tradition was "developed during the long Christian engagement with classical philosophy" and "holds that reason can identify what is best for human beings by studying human nature."[4]

In 1689, Locke published two landmark works he had composed while in exile: the *Essays Concerning Human Understanding* and the *Two Treatises on Government*. In his *Two Treatises*, Locke argued that "natural rights" could be derived from an imagined "state of nature" in which all men were born "independent and equal one amongst the other." In Locke's view, this "natural law" of reason "teaches all Mankind, who would but consult it, that being all equal and independent, no one ought to harm another in his Life, Health, Liberty, or Possessions." Elsewhere Locke reduced the list to three: "life, liberty and property." Inherent to the right to one's own person and possessions was the right to one's own labor:

> Though the earth, and all inferiour creatures, be common to all men, yet every man has a property in his own person: this nobody has any right to but himself. The labour of his body, and the work of his hands, we may say, are properly his.

For Locke, the same applied to those parts of nature with which one "mixed" one's labor. Following the custom of his day, he distinguished between instances of mixing labor and land. Things like hunting and gathering or drawing water from a stream did not imply the separation of land from the commons. But labor that "improved" or "enclosed" the land rendered it private property.[5] This process of "enclosure" was exemplified in Locke's day by the practice of building stone walls to "fence" the land for the harvesting of planted crops or the tending of sheep and cattle. Across succeeding generations, however, this practice would become known by many other terms, such as "acquisition by first use" and "homesteading."[6]

While insisting these concepts derived from the exercise of pure reason, Locke rooted them in his reading of the biblical account of creation, very much shaped by his English Protestant upbringing:

> God and his reason commanded him to subdue the earth, i.e. improve it for the benefit of life, and therein lay out something upon it that was his own, his labour. He that, in obedience to this command of God, subdued, tilled, and sowed any part of it, thereby annexed to it something that was his property, which another had no title to, nor could without injury take from him.[7]

English Protestants on both side of the Atlantic took Locke's argument not as a challenge to Protestant orthodoxy, but rather as a buttress to it. After all, the two great sources of knowledge—the "revelation of Scripture" and the "laws of nature"—were not perceived by faithful Protestants as countervailing forces. On the contrary, they were seen as pushing in the same direction. As Enlightenment thought gained increasing purchase among leading Protestants on both sides of the Atlantic through the course of the eighteenth century, they saw the "natural right" proclaimed by philosophers like John Locke as identical to that scriptural warrant that had been claimed by Puritans like John Cotton. This was the exercise of the "dominion" with which God had endowed human beings in the creation of the world.

A People Numerous and Armed

The first generations of English to colonize North America were oblivious to the fact that their beliefs about land and property were as deeply rooted in ancient English custom as they were in the biblical account of creation or in emerging Enlightenment philosophy. They saw the vast terrains of the "New World" as "wilderness" to which their hardworking labor could be "naturally" mixed. Dutifully, they enclosed family farms and demarcated town limits (in New England, for instance), established parish boundaries and "plantations" (in places like Virginia), and marked colonial perimeters with lookouts and forts. Practices like these seemed utterly logical to English colonists. After all, this was what the orderly use of land looked like.

These practices of landholding were alien to the Native peoples of North America, but the English colonists did not take Native resistance to them as a sign of cultural difference—this way of thinking was centuries in the future. To the English the "Indians" of North America were "heathen"—the word in English derived from the ancient Germanic term *haiphno,* which was the functional equivalent of the Latin word, *paganus.* In early modern English, "heathen" was understood to describe uncivilized human beings who merely wandered in the "heath," or wilderness.[8] Unfamiliar with native practices like seasonal migration, forest husbandry, and tribal hunting, the English saw the Indians of North America as lazy, for they did not dedicate themselves to the hard work of farming as the English knew it. As far as the English were concerned, the Indians' rejection of practices like private landholding and settled agriculture evidenced their need of "civilization." This process required that the Natives should withdraw from the forests and adopt the ways of the English. They should, in short, "settle down" and "get to work."[9]

The Indigenous peoples of North America, meanwhile, experienced the English practice of enclosing land as nonsensical and intrinsically hostile. Many tribes responded to English predations with their own culturally conditioned practices of warfare, among which raid-making and captive-taking would become most notorious among English colonists, as will be detailed in later chapters. Thinking of war as a contest over land, not captives, the English considered these practices inherently diabolical. The legend of peaceful encounter celebrated by Americans at Thanksgiving notwithstanding, conflict grew quickly between New England's Puritan colonizers and the region's Native peoples, rooted in these fundamentally different understandings of the very nature of land. As early as 1645, John Winthrop felt compelled to defend the sustained violence of English colonists in the Massachusetts colony of Plymouth, asserting that they had come "into these parts of the world with desire to advance the kingdom of the Lord Jesus Christ, and to injoye his precious Ordinances with peace." Winthrop considered the conduct of the original colonists to be beyond reproach: "Both in their treaties & converse, they have had an awfull respect to divine rules, endeavouring to walk uprightly and inoffensively, & in the midst of many injuries and instances to exercise much patience and long suffering." However, Winthrop continued, New England's Natives "grew to an excesse of violence and outrage, and proudly turned aside from all wayes of justice and peace, before the sword was drawn or any hostile attempts made against them."[10]

Of course, the Native peoples of New England saw things differently. In 1675, the Wampanoag sachem Metacom complained to Rhode Island governor John Eaton that as far as he was concerned, English colonization was an unrelenting campaign against the Indians—a campaign characterized by "cheating, discrimination, and pressures to sell land, submit to the Plymouth Colony's authority, convert to Christianity and consume alcohol," as Neal Salisbury has summarized.[11] That year, Metacom, known to the English as King Philip, launched an all-out rebellion that lasted over three years and shattered any lingering pretenses of peaceful colonization. In the aftermath of what the English colonists came to call "King Philip's War," their evangelistic aspirations evaporated. An overwhelming consensus emerged among New England elites that their colonial enterprise would need to be prosecuted almost entirely by force.

By 1715 the leading Puritan minister Cotton Mather could casually observe: "The number of Indians in this Land, is not comparable to what it was, in the middle of the former Century. The Wars which after an Offered and Rejected Gospel, they perfidiously began upon the English, above Thirty Years ago, brought a Quick Desolation upon whole Nations of them." Mather interpreted this outcome, matter of factly, as the inevitable outcome of collaboration between the "Bloody Salvages" and "French Priests." The topic of the sermon was "The Death of Good Men, Considered," and the fact that Mather took this topic to encompass only the death of good Englishmen made clear that New England's once ambitious Puritans no longer considered the Native peoples of New England to fall within their evangelical purview.[12]

If the English colonization of North America was a replay of the biblical Exodus—and if therefore the New England colonists were the new Israel—perhaps their destiny was not to convert the Native peoples of North America. Perhaps instead their destiny was to eradicate them, as the Israelites had eradicated the many Canaanite tribes who occupied their "promised land." Perhaps the Native peoples of North America were not heathen to be converted, but rather savages to be conquered. As Kathryn Gin Lum has summarized: "From savable, electable, prodigal brethren whose heathen ignorance could be reversed through the creation of praying towns and other evangelization efforts, Native people became unholy, willfully sinful, demonic Canaanites who deserved, even demanded to be destroyed."[13]

Across the turn of the eighteenth century, this consensus spread among leading colonists in British North America as they engaged in near-perpetual armed conflict with the Native peoples whose lands they were forcibly occupying.

Most commonly, wars in eighteenth-century North America are listed using the names and dates for which they came to be known in retrospect by English colonists—King William's War (1689–97), Queen Anne's War (1702–13), Dummer's War (1722–25), King George's War (1744–48), and so on. But listings like these do the experience only partial justice, for they represent only those occasions when conflict between colonists and native peoples in North America intersected with larger wars between the English Crown and its colonial competitors, the French and the Spanish. In fact, armed conflict in the battle for colonial supremacy was never fully disengaged.

Whether directly, vicariously, or in some combination, generations of English colonists in North America experienced warfare as an ongoing fact of life. They considered the French and the Indians to constitute an existential threat to themselves, their families, their communities, and the entire colonial enterprise. Despite the fact that they were the newcomers in North America, and they were the ones claiming land by force, the English—informed by their very English ways of thinking about the orderly use of land—perceived Indian attacks as unprovoked and unwarranted. This fact of ongoing war shaped the public life of the English colonists at its most elemental level—in the historian John Shy's apt encapsulation, by the simple fact that "almost all white men had guns." By the middle decades of the eighteenth century, the English in North America had become "a people numerous and armed."[14]

The Continental Vision

Across the first half of the eighteenth century, the English colonies in North America were drawn closer together by many and varied means, sometimes by happenstance, sometimes by design, but in ways that were mutually reinforcing. Improved roads and more routinized networks of transportation facilitated more efficient intercolonial exchange of goods and materials of every kind. The rapid growth and racialized hardening of the system of chattel slavery helped to build a vast system of intercolonial trade on which the economies of all the English colonies came to depend.[15] Ties between the colonies were also strengthened by the continued extension of intercolonial networks of correspondence and print production and distribution. The practices of itinerancy and revivalism, embraced by preachers refusing to conform to established boundaries of parish and denomination, birthed intercolonial networks both supporting and opposing new forms of religious expression. Driving all these dynamics was the simple fact of rapid population growth within the English colonies and the continual conquest of native lands.

As they attempted to mark the perimeters of their ever-expanding geographic footprint with networks of forts, outlooks, and patrols, the English encountered constant resistance from Native peoples and from their colonial competitors, the hated Catholic French. For generations, Virginians had found themselves on the front lines of this contest, owing to their voracious appetite for land, which both their growing population and their commitment to the cultivation of tobacco required. In 1585 the lawyer Richard Hakluyt had summarized English aspirations in Virginia this way: "1. To plant Christian religion, 2. To trafficke, 3. To conquer. Or to doe all three."[16] Hakluyt and other early champions of English colonization saw these aspirations as challenging, but not contradictory; rather they would be mutually reinforcing. In 1606, King James I granted the first charter to the Virginia Company of London, permitting them to settle territory in North America that the following year they would name in the king's honor as "Jamestown." This charter included in its stated goals the "propagating of Christian religion to such people, as yet live in darkness and miserable ignorance of the true knowledge and worship of God, and may in time bring the infidels and savages, living in those parts, to human civility, and to a settled and quiet government."[17] Nonetheless, as Annette Gordon-Reed has observed, the Virginia Company "was from the very beginning a money-making enterprise," and in colonial Virginia, "Voracious land grabbing and land speculation, aided and abetted by manipulation of public offices, made a relative handful of people wealthy."[18]

Indeed, by the turn of the eighteenth century, wealthy plantation owners in Virginia almost invariably occupied leading positions in the overlapping county institutions that controlled wealth and power in the colony: they were vestrymen in their county parishes of the Anglican Church, judges or lawyers in their county courts, leaders with rank in the county's regiment of the Virginia Militia, and land surveyors for the county government. Leading men from within each county were also representatives in the colony's House of Burgesses, where they joined forces frequently as officeholders in land-speculating enterprises. In 1748, for instance, the Ohio Company of Virginia was established to advance the prospecting investments of a group of leading landowners that included George Washington.

On May 28, 1754, a foray by men under Washington's command in his position as lieutenant in the Virginia militia resulted in the death of French commander Joseph Coulon de Villiers de Jumonville, near an outlook called "Fort Necessity," located at the eastern perimeter of the Virginia colony. Five weeks later Washington suffered a humiliating defeat at the same site, in what became the first battle in a near-global conflict. Most Europeans would come to call this conflict the "Seven Years' War," although in fact it lasted longer than that. In North America, where the war represented a culmination of fierce colonial competition spanning generations, the English came to call it simply the "French and Indian War." Through the prosecution of this war, leading colonists from across

British North America would begin to fashion for themselves a new self-understanding. This "continental" identity was shaped by shared economic, political, and military interests, to be sure, as well as by a new kind of intercolonial solidarity that was a forerunner of "American" national pride.

At root, however, the "continental" vision that was born among leading English colonists in the great mid-century war reflected a shared desire to expand the territorial bounds of the English colonies—that is, to "enclose" more land. As Woody Holton has carefully chronicled, the colonists who were fighting on the ground in the "backcountry" of North America did not see eye to eye with the English authorities who were charting the course of the wider war from their seats in London. In October 1758, for instance, British officials signed the Treaty of Easton with an alliance of Native tribes in the Upper Ohio Valley, "committing colonists to never again breach the Appalachians." Colonists who had staked their future on ventures like the Ohio Company of Virginia quickly ignored the treaty, however, and "over the objection of British officials set out to advance their claims on western lands."[19]

The conclusion to the war in the early 1760s brought these differences into clear focus. England had acquired vast new territories, and authorities in London had vastly different visions from their American colonists for the future of their relations with the Native peoples of North America. According to Holton, officials in Britain concluded from the war that they "could never defeat France and Spain in North America without Native American allies." Continued territorial expansion by colonists in North America would—as Robert Allison has succinctly summarized—lead to "more conflicts with Native Americans, which would require more troops. To avoid these problems . . . the British crown simply barred white settlement and sale of lands between the Appalachian Mountains and the Mississippi, from Quebec to Florida." In short, leading colonists like George Washington were enraged by British attempts to curtail their territorial expansion and placate Native leaders. After all, they saw their futures—and their fortunes—in the expansive western lands that they called "Ohio."[20]

This resentment about British restraints on the acquisition of Indian land helped bind American colonists together from New England to Virginia. It did so in part because it reflected on a grand scale precisely the same resentments that English colonists expressed toward British authorities about their postwar policies of trade tariffs and taxation. In a speech marking the second anniversary of the March 1770 Boston Massacre, Joseph Warren declared of "the first settlers of this country" that "When they came to this new world, which they fairly purchased of the Indian natives, the only rightful proprietors, they cultivated the then barren soil by their incessant labor, and defended their dear-bought possessions with the fortitude of the Christian, and the bravery of the hero." Warren made clear that the colonists considered taxes and tariffs imposed by British authorities in the aftermath of the French and Indian War not as passing policies affecting colonial enterprise at the margins, but as a standing threat to their most fundamental right, the right of private property.

Referring to his colonial brethren, Warren asked rhetorically, "how can they be said to have PROPERTY" at all, "when a body of men over whom they have not the least controul, and who are not in any way accountable to them, shall oblige them to deliver up any part, or the whole of their substance, without even asking their consent?" Cries of resentment such as these from New Englanders like Warren over British policies of taxation on trade in Boston Harbor resonated powerfully with Virginians like George Washington over British policies threatening to hamstring land-speculating enterprises like the Ohio Company of Virginia.

Order and Violence

The longing for order, shaped by early American Protestant understandings of the natural world, has much to commend it, as can be attested by anyone who has ever lived in a place where disorder prevails. The American commitment to "law and order," to private property, and to the orderly disposition of both private and public lands has given rise to a legal and administrative infrastructure governing land use that compares favorably to that found in many countries across the globe. This commitment can inspire a powerful pride of place, a respect for private property, and a genuine concern for the well-being of neighbor and community. A culture that enshrines these values in law and nourishes complementary practices in individuals helps to provide a foundation for safe, secure, and productive communities across the United States.

But this same longing undergirds a deeply rooted propensity to violence—especially violence over questions of "turf"—that has always characterized American public life. The body politic that would become the United States was conceived in the forcible settlement of Native lands in North America. It was bathed in violence during its period of gestation, marked by the continual prosecution of wars against the French and Indians. And it was birthed in violent insurrection against the authority of the English king. As John Shy observed long ago, "no other nation has had its official origin and constitutional preservation so clearly linked to warfare."[21]

The generations that founded the United States inherited "continental" aspirations from their forefathers. These fueled the practice of continual territorial expansion and the continuous application of force and violence to achieve it. They bequeathed these aspirations—and these associated habits of heart and mind—to their descendants, who acquired tranche after tranche of western lands by a combination of purchase, conquest, occupation, settlement, and broken treaty. Broadly reflecting the desires of their constituents, generations of US presidents embraced this vision wholeheartedly, occupying Native lands through the exercise of sustained and extraordinary violence and exterminating Native peoples as a matter of both policy and practice.

It is not difficult to draw a straight line from this early national history of conquest to the decision by Donald Trump to make a border wall the *de facto* logo of his successful 2016 presidential campaign. The idea of walling off the border resonates powerfully in the imaginations of white people descended from early English colonists, for whom the settlement and "fencing off" of land was a foundational colonizing strategy. The idea of building a "big, beautiful wall" to "secure" our nation's southern border seems to hold out the promise that someday Americans will finally succeed in "enclosing" the continent. The taproot of this tradition of territorial conquest—the deep, often unconscious, way of thinking that served to rationalize centuries of land grabs—was what early English Protestants understood to be the essential work of bringing order to the wilderness of North America. Millions of white Americans today harbor this ancient prejudice that the darker peoples who live outside our borders are inherently wild and savage.

Neither is it hard to draw a straight line from the violence that was intrinsic to the American founding and the continued pervasive violence that characterizes American public life today. The United States remains an utter outlier among the nations of the world in deaths by firearm for two simple reasons. The first is that Americans own so many more guns than people in other nations—we are still "a people numerous and armed."[22] And the second reason is that so many Americans are trained from childhood to "defend your turf" and "stand your ground." Many Americans take these commands as clear warrant for the exercise of violence in the defense of territorial boundaries.

American men are especially prone to this expansive under-standing of property rights. On February 26, 2012, George Zimmerman, a neighborhood watch coordinator in a gated community of Sanford, Florida, confronted an unarmed Black seventeen-year-old, Trayvon Martin, who was visiting relatives nearby. After an ensuing struggle, Zimmerman shot Martin to death. He was later acquitted of second-degree murder charges after arguing he shot Martin in self-defense. Ten years later, in the same Florida town, two white men accosted a Black sixteen-year-old, Jermaine Jones, who was speeding in their neighborhood. After throwing a traffic cone at the car, and then a brick through one of its windows, the men grew enraged when the young driver got out of his car and started recording the encounter on his cellphone. After one accused Jones of "burning out racing through my fucking neighborhood," the other approached the teen, insisting, "I'm not in your face. Get out of my neighborhood." After starting to record the confron-tation on her own cellphone, a white woman reinforced the message: "Get out of our neighborhood. You don't belong here."[23]

Some young white American men take this propensity to violence to its most horrifying extremes, the extremes of vigi-lantism and mass shooting. So, Kyle Rittenhouse, a seventeen-year-old from Antioch, Illinois, felt compelled to travel to nearby Kenosha, Wisconsin, on August 25, 2020, when civil unrest broke out there after the fatal police shooting two days earlier of a twenty-nine-year-old Black man, Jacob Blake. Armed with an AR-15, Rittenhouse was confronted by protesters, and responded by killing two and injuring a third. Rittenhouse was acquitted on the grounds that he acted in self-defense. And so, Payton Gendron, a white eighteen-year-old living in Buffalo, searched by zip code in May 2022 for a neighborhood with the highest concentration of Black people so that he could "kill as many blacks as possible," the number of which turned out to be ten.[24] The victims of these crimes were all Black, a matter that will be addressed in chapter 3. But they were also victims of young white men who conceived of themselves as defending their turf.

When I read of the Buffalo shooting while writing this book, I was reminded of a visit many years ago to an old friend of the family, who was living now in upstate New Hampshire. This friend lived with his wife in a small rural town, in a lovely three-bedroom home on an acre of land bordered at the back by forest. As a part of his genuine and ritualized expressions of hospitality, he assured me that he was well-armed and that should anyone harbor designs to trespass on his property, they would get what was coming to them. Considering how bad crime had gotten lately—something he had heard confirmed again and again "on the news"—he had also recently purchased his wife a handgun and trained her in its use. For the first time in her life, she was now carrying a firearm in her purse everywhere she went. My old friend shared all this with me in a casual tone that made clear he knew I would understand where he was coming from. It was clear he assumed I would find his family's preparedness to resort to violence reassuring. There we sat, two white men chatting amiably and comfortably, looking out the window toward the back of the yard and into the thick of the forest.

But when I returned to my own comfortable home in suburban San Diego, I had to wonder whether I was so different from my old family friend, whose political views and cultural posture I found so repugnant. While I have never and will never own a firearm, I, too, live in a predominantly white community, in a comfortable home with a fenced backyard. Years ago, my wife and I chose this community—as do so many young white Americans—for its secure, quiet neighborhoods and its quality public schools. We were able to buy into this neighborhood because my parents helped us with the down payment on a mortgage, something they were able to do because my father (wisely) invested in California real estate beginning in the 1970s and because his father (wisely) purchased farmlands in Kansas beginning in the 1930s. But prior to that the Fanestil family land was acquired by more than the application of wisdom and labor.

My paternal ancestors were "Volga Germans"—so called because they arrived from the Volga River Valley of Russia, where they had lived in German enclaves for up to a century. Thousands of Volga Germans moved to Kansas in the 1860s and 1870s. Some purchased parcels of land from railroad companies who were eager to settle the territories their new railways would traverse. But other Volga Germans acquired their lands by "homesteading," a practice by which whites in the western territories of the United States routinely settled land without purchasing it. This practice continued long after the provisions of the 1862 Homestead Act had expired, and white settlers took advantage of it well beyond the formal provisions of the law. I don't know whether my great-great-grandfather purchased or homesteaded the first land he came to own in northwestern Kansas. In either case, the establishment of communities like his was made possible by standing policies and practices of the US federal government in the late nineteenth century, which encouraged white settlement of western lands. At this same time the federal government was continuing to actively dispossess Native peoples of their ancestral lands and was walking back the promises it had made to emancipated slaves at the end of the Civil War—including the promise of "forty acres and a mule." Like millions of white Americans, I am the inheritor of accumulated wealth made possible by what William Darity has described as "a host of social policies and practices that were put in place in the aftermath of the Civil War," beginning with "the failure to provide the formerly enslaved with the 40 acre land grants that they were promised, at the same time substantial allocations of land were being made to white Americans."[25]

The reach of this American brand of white-settler colonialism is longer still. The comfortable neighborhood that we enjoy was made possible by a vast system of interstate highways, constructed at public expense in the mid-twentieth century, connecting suburban communities like ours to San Diego's urban center. To facilitate this construction, the state of California subdivided urban neighborhoods through the exercise of eminent domain—the forcible seizing of land. In doing so it uprooted thousands of residents in San Diego's historic Mexican American barrio, and thousands more in the predominantly African American neighborhoods of the city's southeast quadrant. At the time, "restrictive covenants" were still in place in San Diego's predominantly white suburbs like the one I grew up in, and mortgage companies almost uniformly practiced "redlining," ensuring that the city—like all major American cities—would remain profoundly segregated.[26] Urban land use policies are not as discriminatory as they once were, and formally racist practices are no longer sanctioned by law, but studies show that unequal practices in mortgage lending and apartment rentals remain widespread. Meanwhile, the prevailing popularity of so-called NIMBY movements ("not in my backyard") continues to make it difficult to construct low-income housing in neighborhoods like mine.[27]

It is easy and accurate for me to conclude that the English who colonized North America, including revolutionaries like George Washington, succumbed to the temptations of white Christian nationalism, an American heresy. It is easy for me to conclude the same about my distant family friend in upstate New Hampshire. But my life of privilege, too, has been shaped by the enduring and pernicious reach of this American heresy.

CHAPTER 2

Providence
Destiny and Nostalgia

For early English Protestants, the Bible told a single coherent story from front to back. God had spoken the whole of creation into being and then created humankind to play a special role in it. As punishment for Adam's "fall," the power of sin and the punishment of death had been passed down through every human generation. God sought to redeem humankind through a "chosen" nation, the nation of Israel, but the Jews had proven to be a stubborn people, refusing even to heed the Prophets, messengers sent by God. Determined to conquer the powers of sin and death, God took on human flesh in the person of Jesus and through his self-sacrifice offered the "deliverance of salvation" to all the nations of the earth. Human history from this point forward was the story of this gospel's spread, by which the good news of what God had done in Jesus Christ would be shared to every corner of the earth. Its fulfillment would come at "the end of days," when Christ would return to rule over all creation.

In this early English Protestant way of thinking, the whole of history could be found within the pages of the Bible. God was the author both of "the Good Book" and of the history it contained. Most commonly, English Protestants called this governing function of God's nature "Providence."

A providential view of divine agency affords its adherents a kind of all-purpose escape hatch in interpreting the human experience. When events conform nicely to expectations,

the faithful can embrace them as clear signs of divine inter-
vention and as affirmations of their proper place in human
history. But when events fail to meet expectations, they can
take refuge in the belief that someday, in hindsight, everything
will be seen to have worked together in a divinely orchestrated
plan. Individually and collectively, defeats, disappointments,
and confusion do not reflect the limitations of divine agency,
nor the fallibility of the sacred cause. Rather, they reflect the
meager understanding of mere mortals.

This way of thinking remains a powerful force in American
culture, as will be understood by anyone who has ever been
consoled in the face of hardship with words like "everything
happens for a reason." At a national level, this understanding is
manifest in the belief that God has granted the United States a
unique (and benevolent) role in human history—a belief shared
by more than six in ten Americans.[1] This belief is so deeply
rooted in American culture that calling the United States "the
greatest nation on earth" remains a virtual prerequisite for
politicians of every party who aspire to hold national office.
Expressions like this can evoke a powerful sense of purpose and
aspiration. They can also conjure longing and nostalgia, habits
of heart and mind that have always characterized American
public life and continue to do so today.

The Doctrine of Providence

Early English Protestants understood that God's very being
is eternal and God's power absolute. This understanding was
reinforced continually by the Church of England's "Common
Prayer." Developed across generations and compiled into an
authoritative edition by Protestant authorities in 1662, the
Book of Common Prayer declared in its very first "Article of
Religion": "There is but one living and true God, everlasting,
without body, parts, or passions; of infinite power, wisdom,
and goodness; the maker and preserver of all things both
visible and invisible."[2] Each Sunday for centuries in Anglican

parishes across the English-speaking world, the faithful spoke the Apostles' Creed aloud together, beginning with this declaration: "I believe in one God the Father Almighty, Maker of heaven and earth, And of all things visible and invisible."

As a rule, early English Protestants who dissented from Anglican orthodoxy were even more devoted to the doctrine of providence. By their reading, the Scriptures spoke clearly of God's supreme majesty, or "sovereignty." In 1678 John Flavel summed this view up in the opening lines of his *Divine Conduct: The Mystery of Providence*: "The greatness of God is a glorious and unsearchable mystery." Flavel had been ejected in 1662 from his Church of England pulpit for "nonconformity," but he continued to meet secretly with his parishioners in defiance of the Conventicle Act of 1664, which banned non-Anglican religious assemblies of more than five people. Flavel's writings—chief among them his *Divine Conduct*—would prove enduringly popular among generations of Protestant clergy on both sides of the Atlantic. As he saw it, "the affairs of the saints in this world are certainly conducted by the wisdom and care of a special Providence." And the purview of providence was absolute: "It has not only its hand in this or that, but in all that concerns them. It has its eyes upon everything that relates to them throughout their lives, from first to last."

The unceasing care of providence did not exempt the faithful from suffering, Flavel explained, but rather shepherded them through it, much as God provided the distressed people of Israel safe passage through the Red Sea, or as God delivered Daniel from the lion's den (Daniel 3:22), or as Jesus sent out his disciples like "sheep in the midst of wolves" (Matthew 10:16). The truly faithful should not aspire to understand the workings of providence, Flavel insisted. Rather, they should rejoice in the "marvelous coincidences of Providence, confederating and greeting, as it were, to meet and unite themselves to bring about the good of God's chosen." Deploying a metaphor commonly associated with "Deistic" thinking that would begin to spread in the eighteenth century, he compared the course of human history to the intricate workings of an elaborate time-piece. From this side of eternity, human beings were consigned to seeing only "the disjointed wheels and scattered pins of a watch," not "the whole united in one frame." Only in eternity would a full understanding of these coincidences become clear to those who had been delivered safely into the celestial realm. As Flavel put it: "O what a delightful sight that will be, to behold, at one view, the whole design of Providence, and the proper place and use of every single act, which we could not understand in this world."[3]

Practices of corporate worship were especially influential in shaping understandings of divine providence among devout English Protestants. English Puritans, the most strident of all in this regard, rejected altogether the Anglican practices of Common Prayer and choral liturgy, for which they could find no warrant in the Bible. Instead, they opted to sing only psalms, and without instrumental accompaniment, a practice that came to be known as "lining out" the psalms. Over time they embraced "metrical" singing, translating the psalms into metered verse to allow for more coordinated congregational singing. The result was a manner of singing that induced a corporate, almost trance-like, experience in which the singers were encouraged to imagine that they were joining a heavenly chorus.[4] Those participating in the Puritan tradition of psalm-singing were routinely encouraged to consider their place within the larger sweep of God's spatial and temporal majesty. As reflected in the opening lines of one of their favorite Psalms:

> Lord, thou hast been our dwelling place in all generations.
> Before the mountains were brought forth, or ever thou hadst formed the earth and the world, even from everlasting to everlasting, thou art God. (Psalm 90:1–2, KJV)

A profound awareness of the vulnerability of the human condition was tempered by a conviction that God's benevolent and eternal reign allowed a special protection for even ordinary human beings.

Succeeding generations of Puritans on both sides of the Atlantic sustained this essential spirit through the practice of corporate singing while loosening restrictions on it. Over time, they created more lyrical translations of the psalms, incorporated the use of musical instruments (typically the organ), and expanded their repertoires of metered verse. Isaac Watts was immersed from childhood in this musical tradition and became its most prolific innovator. Born in Southampton, England, in 1674, Watts was raised in a devout and noncon-forming family and educated at institutions established by Christians dissenting from Anglican orthodoxy. Beginning at the turn of the eighteenth century, Watts introduced new trans-lations of the psalms and a new genre of "spiritual songs" that revolutionized the practice of metrical singing across the entire spectrum of English-language Protestantism. His rendering of Psalm 90 would become the most enduringly popular hymn in the English-speaking world:

> Our God our help in ages past
> Our hope for years to come
> Our shelter from the stormy blast
> And our eternal home.
>
> Under the shadow of Thy throne
> Thy saints have dwelt secure;
> Sufficient is Thine arm alone,
> And our defense is sure.
>
> Before the hills in order stood
> Or earth received her frame,
> From everlasting Thou art God
> To endless years the same.[5]

Watts's enormously popular *Divine Songs Attempted in Easy Language for the Use of Children* reflected this same sense of double awe—awe at the sheer majesty of God's creation and awe that human beings held a special place in it. For instance, this song, originally entitled "Praise for Creation and Providence," would become best known by its opening line and remain popular among English-speaking Protestants for centuries:

> I Sing th'Almighty Pow'r of GOD,
> That made the Mountains rise,
> That spread the flowing Seas abroad,
> And built the lofty Skies. . . .

> His Hand is my perpetual Guard,
> He keeps me with his Eye:
> Why should I then forget the Lord
> Who is for ever nigh?[6]

Watts's lyrics combined reason and feeling, enlightenment wonder at the natural world and pietistic Protestant devotion. Their enormous popularity in North America spanned denominational, geographic, and racial-cultural bounds, binding English-speaking Protestants together in a shared experience of celebrating God's providence in song—and training the young to perceive that their own lives were caught up in the divine sweep of "Providence."[7]

The Promise of Divine Protection

The Puritans who first settled colonies in what they called "New England" believed their endeavors were expressions of grand providential designs. Early New Englanders like William Bradford frequently compared their experience to that of the twelve tribes of Israel, who were liberated from captivity in ancient Egypt by God's mighty hand and were likewise delivered into the "promised land" of Canaan. Reflecting on the experience of the *Mayflower* "Pilgrims" who established the

Plymouth colony after arriving on Cape Cod in 1620, Bradford compared their crossing of the Atlantic to the Israelites' crossing of the Red Sea: "Our fathers were Englishmen which came over this great ocean . . . let them which have been redeemed of the Lord, show how he hath delivered them from the hand of the oppressor."[8] Generations of English preachers in North America would follow Bradford's lead and proclaim the English colonial enterprise—and, later, the nation of the United States—to be a "new Israel."

This belief did not exempt the New England colonists from struggle and conflict, but it did afford them the frame through which they could interpret the twists and turns of history that made their survival possible. Reflecting on the word "welcome" that the Massasoit Indian Samoset uttered to a delegation of Pilgrims on March 16, 1621—a word he had learned from previous encounters with English fishermen—Bradford recalled years later in his memoirs that Samoset also "told us that about four years ago all the inhabitants died of an extraordinary plague, and there is neither man, woman, nor child remaining . . . to hinder our possession, or to lay claim unto it." Bradford acknowledged that things might have been different had the Massasoit not been "reduced down to three hundred." As it was, he observed, "out of the bosom of death came that refreshing word, 'welcome.'"[9]

The English welcome in New England was short-lived, of course, but the first generations of colonists interpreted this, too, through the Bible story of the Exodus. Just as Joshua and the conquering Israelites had to contend with the residents of Canaan as they occupied their "promised land," so did the New Englanders face the daunting threat posed by North America's Native peoples. This was exemplified by the threat of Indian captivity, fears of which in early New England grew out of all proportion to the actual risk. In 1682 the Puritan minister Joseph Rowlandson published the autobiographical account of his wife, Mary, who six years earlier had been taken captive by Wampanoag Indians. *The Sovereignty and Goodness of God . . . Being a Narrative of the Captivity and Restauration of Mrs. Mary Rowlandson, a Minister's Wife in New-England* resonated powerfully across the colonies, lending itself to the same kind of allegorical reading by which readers were accustomed to interpreting their Bibles. Beginning with Rowlandson's account, what later generations of historians would call the "Indian captivity narratives" became the most popular homegrown form of literature in British North America—precursors, of sorts, to the tales of horror and suspense marketed so successfully to today's teens in movies and books.

The most popular narratives told the tales of English colonists who were taken captive but then providentially returned to their communities through acts of warfare or exchange. The experiences of these "redeemed" captives were seen as representing the colonial experience writ large—like the kidnapped colonists themselves, the English colonies might be taken temporarily "captive" by dark spiritual forces, but hope sprang eternal that their noble enterprise could be restored.[10] Straight through to the end of the eighteenth century, English clergy and printers collaborated to replenish the stock of captivity narratives with new additions, even as traditional favorites enjoyed long runs of continuous republication. This constant flow reinforced a composite narrative: the providential destiny of the English was divinely sanctioned; the aspirations of the French and the collaboration of Native peoples were diabolically inspired.

New England's Puritan leaders also identified with the Hebrew prophets, as they grew alarmed by the wayward—which is to say human—conduct of their congregations. Convinced that some from among their own number had strayed from God's covenant with them, they found special inspiration in the prophet Jeremiah, who announced the judgment of God on the nation of Judah:

> Thus saith the LORD; I remember thee, the kindness of thy youth, the love of thine espousals, when thou wentest after me in the wilderness, in a land that was not sown. . . . I brought you into a plentiful country, to eat the fruit thereof and the goodness thereof; but when ye entered, ye defiled my land, and made mine heritage an abomination. (Jeremiah 2:2, 5, 7, KJV)

Following Jeremiah's pattern, Puritan preachers began to warn their congregants that their lack of faith and many failings threatened both their own eternal salvation and the larger New England experiment. In his 1671 sermon, "A Brief Recognition of New England's Errand into the Wilderness," Samuel Danforth, pastor of the Puritan congregation in Roxbury, Massachusetts, acknowledged as inevitable that some were "apt in time to abate and cool in their affection" but cautioned that these ought "seriously and thoroughly to examine themselves." Challenging his listeners (and readers) to contrast themselves with the first congregations in New England, Danforth asked: "Who is there left among you, that saw these Churches in their first glory, and how do you see them now? Are they not in your eyes in comparison thereof, as nothing? How is the gold become dim! how is the most fine gold changed!"

The Puritan "jeremiads" are most notorious for their harsh and scolding rhetoric, but sermons like Danforth's were simultaneously backward and forward looking. They contrasted the present not with an ancient past, but with a past that had not yet quite slipped from memory, allowing for the possibility that it could yet be reclaimed, reconjured, rekindled, and restored. Indeed, the prophet Jeremiah himself had held out hope of restoration, extending a divine invitation—"Return, ye backsliding children, and I will heal your backslidings"—and then responding on behalf of the people: "Behold, we come unto thee; for thou art the LORD our God" (Jeremiah 3:22, KJV). Likewise, the preachers of early New England jeremiads did not leave their congregants without remedy. As Danforth put it: "If the people cleave to the Lord, to his Prophets, and to his Ordinances, it will strike such a fear into the hearts of enemies, that they will be at their wits ends, and not know what to do.... In this way we have the promise of divine Protection and Preservation."[11]

In an odd way, it was the precipitousness of decline that seemed to fuel the promise of Puritan renewal. God had ordained the English colonial enterprise—this was never called into question—and yet the promises inherent in this divine "election" were not being fulfilled in the lives of the New England colonists. Continued hardship, deprivation, and suffering could not reflect the failings of an infallible God. Rather, the people themselves must have failed to fulfill their obligations—or, more precisely, some among them must have done. The diagnosis and remedy to the travails of the English in North America seemed abundantly clear: a wholesale spiritual and cultural renewal was needed precisely because the present generation had fallen so far and so fast. But this also meant the golden days could be recovered, precisely because they were not so far gone.

A Common and Glorious Cause

While widely and correctly associated with New England's Puritans, the belief that the English colonial enterprise was divinely sanctioned would come to be shared by almost all English Protestants in colonial North America. As George McKenna summarized in his 2007 *The Puritan Origins of American Patriotism*, the Puritans' providential vision of America made for "an attractive story and a very adaptable one because it would be creatively reinterpreted in a variety of ways.

Its geographical source was New England, but the movement of New England's large and ethnically homogeneous population, the compactness of its culture, and the enormous volume of New England writings—books, sermons, periodicals, and newspapers—insured the Puritan narrative reached a colony wide audience." Across the course of the eighteenth century, McKenna argues, a broad intercolonial consensus emerged from this Puritan narrative, leading the English in North America to conclude that they were "a people set apart, a people with a providential mission."[12]

As it was in so many other respects, their near-perpetual war with the French and the Indians was a critical catalyst to this new intercolonial self-understanding. Across the first half of the eighteenth century, aggressive policies of forcible expansion into what the English called "Indian Country" led the colonists to seek what they called "common cause" with one another, over and against their Native enemies and colonial competitors. As Robert Parkinson has chronicled, this phrase had deep roots, stretching back generations as "a vague call to Protestants to join forces against their religious foes, whether Catholic or Muslims."[13] The French and Indian War helped to cement the understanding among leading English colonists that their distinctly Protestant destiny had indeed been divinely ordained. Samuel Bird summed things up neatly in the opening lines of a sermon delivered in New Haven on April 27, 1759, "to Colonel David Wooster and His Company, at the Request of the Colonel":

> War is in its self very undesirable; but nevertheless, it is some Times an indispensable Duty, or absolute Necessity, and of great Importance to undertake it. A just War is rather to be chosen, then an unjust Peace.[14]

For English colonists, the great mid-century war was not merely a war of colonial conquest over the French and the Indians—it was a just war and a holy undertaking precisely because it was so clearly a Protestant cause.

In the aftermath of the French and Indian War, leaders from across the colonies—and from across the theological spectrum—embraced the understanding, as Thomas Kidd has summarized, that Britain "had abandoned its providential role, descending into corruption and evil."[15] In the buildup to the American Revolution, colonial leaders routinely asserted that a new nation was being called forth by God to pick up this fallen mantle. Indeed, this conviction that God had established the English colonies in North America for a special purpose was almost universally shared by leading figures from the American Revolution. In 1772, the town leaders of Boston voted unanimously to publish at public expense a poem by James Allen, which opened with these lines:

> From realms of bondage and a Tyrant's reign,
> Our Godlike Fathers bore no slavish chain,
> To Pharaoh's face th' inspired Patriarchs stood,
> To seal their virtue, with a Martyr's blood:
> But lives so precious such a sacred seed,
> The sources of empires, Heaven's high will decreed;
> He snatch'd the SAINTS from Pharaoh's impious hand,
> And bid his chosen seek this distant land.[16]

Leading Bostonians who delivered annual orations marking the anniversary of the March 1770 Boston Massacre conjured this same story, as for instance did Joseph Warren when he delivered the oration for the second time, in 1775:

> Our fathers, having nobly resolved never to wear the yoke of despotism . . . determined to find a place in which they might enjoy their freedom, or perish in the glorious attempt. Approving Heaven beheld the favourite ark dancing upon the waves, and graciously preserved it until the chosen families were brought in safety to these western regions.

Warren reduced the entire history of New England to a divinely sanctioned and just war of conquest:

> Having become the honest proprietors of the soil, they immediately applied themselves to the cultivation of it, and they soon beheld the virgin earth teeming with richest fruits. . . . The savage natives saw with wonder the delightful change, and quickly formed a scheme to obtain that by fraud or force, which nature meant as the reward of industry alone. But the illustrious emigrants soon convinced the rude invaders that they were not less ready to take the field for battle than for labour; and the insidious foe was driven from their borders as often as he ventured to disturb them.[17]

Across a century and a half, the native peoples of North America had been transformed in the imagination of English colonists from the welcoming sufferers of a catastrophic plague into "savages" and "rude invaders" who got what they deserved.

Leaders of the Continental Congresses routinely embraced this core conviction that the revolutionary cause was linked intrinsically to the cause of Protestant colonization. The Rev. Jacob Duché, rector of Christ Church Anglican parish in Philadelphia, opened the first session of the Continental Congress on September 7, 1774, with a prayer that was so well received it earned him an invitation to stay on as the Congress's permanent chaplain. The prayer began this way:

> O Lord our Heavenly Father, high and mighty King of kings, and Lord of lords, who dost from Thy throne behold all the dwellers on earth and reignest with power supreme and uncontrolled over all the Kingdoms, Empires and Governments; look down in mercy, we beseech Thee, on these our American States, who have fled to Thee from the rod of the oppressor and thrown themselves on Thy gracious protection, desiring to be henceforth dependent only on Thee.[18]

Congress reinforced this message through its continual practice of public prayer, through the hosting of funeral sermons
for its own members, and by hosting memorial commemorations of many different kinds, including days of public
prayer. When Congress declared July 20, 1775, "a day of public
HUMILIATION, FASTING, and PRAYER," it issued a general
proclamation recognizing "the GREAT GOVERNOR of the
WORLD," who "by his supreme and universal Providence,
not only conducts the course of nature with unerring wisdom
and rectitude, but frequently influences the minds of men
to serve the wise and gracious purposes of His providencial
Government."[19] The proclamation was printed and distributed
throughout the colonies.

Clergy played an indispensable role in promoting this same
conviction, working in close collaboration with members
of Congress and leaders of the Continental Army. American
preachers worked assiduously to connect the revolutionary
cause in the hearts and minds of their followers to the providential legacy inherited from prior generations. To cite just
one of countless examples, in a sermon preached in Yorktown
on the General Fast Day in 1775, Daniel Batwell exhorted two
companies of riflemen to go on to their "appointed destination,
in the fear of God, in the sentiments of true honor, in the love
of Liberty and of their Country." Addressing them directly he
expressed his confidence that "you have not degenerated from
their nobleness of soul, but will even strive to exceed your forefathers in deeds of valour, generosity and humanity." Declaring
that "a glorious cause is put into your hands," he exhorted
them to "offer up our supplications to the allwise, omnipo-
tent, and merciful Disposer of all events," in order "That these
Colonies may be ever under the care and protection of a kind
Providence."[20]

But it was not just the most religious among America's
revolutionary generation who saw themselves as the rightful
inheritors of the providential role abandoned by Great Britain.

After completing their work on the committee that drafted the Declaration of Independence, Benjamin Franklin and Thomas Jefferson—known today as among the least devout of the Founding Fathers—continued their work of branding the new nation by embracing a familiar theme. For the nation's new seal Franklin proposed a scene from the biblical story of the Exodus, including a representation of its most iconic moment, the parting of the Red Sea.[21]

In the aftermath of their successful revolution, Americans worked collaboratively to consecrate the new nation as having been birthed through providential design. This work unfolded across generations and conjured a spirit of perpetual remembrance and nostalgia. In 1831, a student at Andover Theological Seminary summed things up in a lyrical form reflecting the style of Isaac Watts. Samuel Francis Smith's composition would function for generations as the *de facto* national anthem of the United States, until "The Star-Spangled Banner" began to be widely used in the late nineteenth century. The lyrics conjure the majesty of God's creation, the pure motives of the English who first colonized North America, and the providential founding of the United States:

> My country, 'tis of thee,
> Sweet land of liberty,
> Of thee I sing;
> Land where my fathers died,
> Land of the pilgrims' pride,
> From ev'ry mountainside
> Let freedom ring!
>
> My native country, thee,
> Land of the noble free,
> Thy name I love;
> I love thy rocks and rills,
> Thy woods and templed hills;
> My heart with rapture thrills,
> Like that above.

Let music swell the breeze,
And ring from all the trees
Sweet freedom's song;
Let mortal tongues awake;
Let all that breathe partake;
Let rocks their silence break,
The sound prolong.

Our fathers' God to Thee,
Author of liberty,
To Thee we sing.
Long may our land be bright,
With freedom's holy light,
Protect us by Thy might,
Great God our King![22]

Ensuing generations of white Americans embraced and cele-brated this collective self-understanding of providential destiny, as suggested by the banner they hung over their west-ward expansion. Americans understood their "continental" destiny to be "manifest," meaning evident, obvious, apparent, or plain. In the white American understanding of things, their destiny was all these things because it could be traced back so obviously to the founding of the new nation, and from there to the Protestant colonization of the New World.

Destiny and Nostalgia

The fact that things did not go as planned for the first generations of English who colonized New England drove successive generations to search for explanations. As they conjured and romanticized their past, the aim of New England's Puritan pastors became clear: to restore the sense of purpose and destiny they believed their forefathers had embodied. Their sermonic jeremiads gave powerful expres-sion to this fear of lost promise and to a nostalgic longing for the restoration of what they romanticized as a golden age. Across the first half of the eighteenth century, English colonists throughout North America were inspired not just by their growing thirst for greater economic and political self-determination but also by this conviction that they were fulfilling grand and providential designs. The early generations of English colonists who conjured this powerful mix of backward-looking nostalgia and forward-looking aspiration had not yet embraced for themselves the identity of "Americans"—that moniker did not begin to spread until the mid-eighteenth century. But if they had, they would have said what was needed was to make America great again.

On the one hand, all this is a very natural process by which national identities are fashioned and formed and transmitted down through the generations. Ritualized acts of commemoration, the practiced rehearsal of founding narratives, the careful attention paid to teaching these narratives to the young—these are common practices among all the nations of the earth. As the historian David Blight has framed it, the enterprise of nation-building requires the construction not just of geographic boundaries—it also requires reshaping "the malleable topography of memory."[23] In this sense, nostalgia is an indispensable part of statecraft.

But there is a dark side to the specific kind of nostalgia that is the spiritual inheritance of Americans descended from the colonizing tradition of early English Protestantism. In the last chapter we saw how, across centuries, white Americans shaped by the traditions of early English Protestantism have been prone to organize, arm, and prepare themselves to defend what they believe to be their turf. But as far as many white Americans are concerned, it is the "malleable topography of memory" that most needs defending. Opponents of what they call "critical race theory" have now passed what Keeanga-Yamahtta Taylor has aptly characterized as "a frenzy of legislation sharply limiting the ways that slavery, and other aspects of America's racist history, can be discussed in schools—or whether they can be discussed at all."[24] Just as the early Puritans were tempted to romanticize the first generations of New England colonists, so white Americans today are tempted to want to "enclose" the past.

That the first colonists to settle in New England were a "new Israel," that the American Revolution was ordained by God, that the subsequent enterprise of nation-building was part of grand providential designs—all this makes for a compelling story. White Protestants are the heroes of this traditional story, and it is only natural that many white Protestants today feel threatened by attempts to complicate it. Some find talk of "deconstructing" American history and "decolonizing" the American public square so bewildering they simply assume that they must be born from sinister motives aimed knowingly at mass deception.[25] After all, everyone knows that the real American history is the American history that real Americans know.

But all this is the easy part to see. Harder for progressive white Americans to recognize is how we also have fallen prey to the temptation of nostalgia, creating our own preferred narrative of American history. By this narrative we grant ourselves permission to identify always and everywhere with the heroes in the story. Sure, a sense of providential destiny gave ideological support for the institution of slavery, we say, but it also shaped Abraham Lincoln's conviction that the United States represented "the last best hope of earth."[26] Protestant providentialism sanctioned the genocide of Native peoples under the banner of "Manifest Destiny," and Protestant nostalgia fueled the "Lost Cause" of the Confederacy, but this spiritual inheritance also fueled the Progressive movement of the late nineteenth century and the Social Gospel movement of the early twentieth.[27] A gut-level conviction that America was favored by God helped to fan the flames of virulent anti-immigrant sentiment in the late nineteenth and early twentieth centuries, but it also sustained the zeal of many American soldiers through two world wars in the fight against European fascism. We who are white and Christian and progressive like to take selective strolls through our personal and denominational histories, attaching ourselves only to the progressive or prophetic strands of our traditions.

Likewise, we are reluctant to accept that our spiritual inheritance is shaped by the white racism that was endemic to American Protestantism throughout most of its history. We mock conservative Christians who misappropriate a single quote from Martin Luther King Jr.—"I have a dream that my four little children will one day live in a nation where they will not be judged by the color of their skin but by the content of their character"—to mischaracterize him as somehow "color blind."[28] But we are inclined to cherry-pick Dr. King ourselves. Our favorite quotation—"The arc of the moral universe is long, but it bends toward justice"—sheds almost as little light on the whole of King's teaching, and it too is plucked out of the context in which King deployed it.[29] It is no coincidence that this quotation is palatable to progressive politicians because it allows them to evoke the providentialism so endemic to American culture.

When the subjects of privilege and prejudice are broached, most of us who count ourselves as liberal-minded white Christians are quick to distinguish ourselves from the most illiberal views of some of our Christian coreligionists. "I am the other kind of Christian," I have said on more than one occasion, in response to someone asking me about racism, sexism, and homophobia in the Christian Church.

But am I? By condemning the existence of white Christian nationalism in other branches of the Christian family tree, and by choosing to identify myself so strongly with only the liberating strands of American Christianity, I avoid the hard work of examining my own heritage, my own tradition, my own family, and myself. My finger-pointing amounts to a sleight of hand, a kind of "whataboutism" that allows me to avoid self-reflection by shifting the focus onto others. By presuming that the course of American history runs on an arc that bends toward justice, and by presuming that this is the arc that describes my life, I ignore another possibility: that the United States was founded as a Herrenvolk society, that the "master race" dynamics of this founding are still very much at work in our public life, and that I am both an inheritor and a practitioner of wealth and privilege.

In seeking to exonerate myself, I become like the well-meaning moderate white Christians whom Martin Luther King Jr. described in his "Letter from a Birmingham Jail" as living "behind the anesthetizing security of stained-glass windows."[30] A better role model for white American Christians like me would be Edward Ball, who unflinchingly confronted the slaveholding past of his ancestors. Almost all of us who are white in America have had "Slaves in the Family."[31]

As it turns out, all white Christians in America are perpetually tempted by the blinding power of this distinctly American brand of nostalgia, derived from a deep-rooted belief in an early English Protestant form of providence. This spiritual inheritance has been passed down to us across many generations and can be rightly traced to the founding of the early Puritan colonies in New England. Oblivious to the fact their ways were culturally conditioned, the first English to arrive in North America were slow to understand and quick to demonize their erstwhile neighbors. Longing to fulfill the dreams of their forebears, succeeding generations of English in North America barely paused to consider how their own sense of destiny might trample the aspirations of others. This white Christian nationalist brand of American nostalgia renders us prone to romanticize our own collective pasts and tempts us perpetually to overlook how what John Flavel called "the mystery of Providence" may be at work in other peoples.

CHAPTER 3

Salvation
Progress and White Racism

While they often interpreted it very differently, early English Protestants agreed that the Bible's final book, Revelation, foretold the "end of days," a time beyond time when those who found favor with Christ would live with him for all time and when those who did not would live in an eternal state of torment and damnation. This dualistic way of thinking about the dimension of eternity meant that, as far as devout Protestants were concerned, a fundamental spiritual question confronted every human being in this life: "What must I do to be saved?"[1] For early English Protestants, this question was not distant or abstract, because neither was the reality of death. To the contrary, they experienced death as a perpetual threat—at a moment's notice, anyone could be called to "meet their Maker."

The threat of eternal damnation was the source of much anxiety in the English Protestant soul. Grounding their views in the writings of the Apostle Paul, Protestant leaders encouraged their followers to resolve this anxiety by trusting that "all things work together for good to them that love God" (Romans 8:28, KJV). Paul's views were clearly shaped by the Greek philosophical tradition of "teleology"—the notion that human endeavors are shaped by their ultimate purpose or final aim. Across centuries a broad consensus emerged among English Protestants. The proper remedy to the uncertainties of life was not the passive reliance on God's initiative, but rather active participation in God's purposeful designs. Even the smallest actions of ordinary daily living might be signs of redemption. The truly faithful were those who determined to "work out their own salvation" (Philippians 2:12, KJV).

English Protestant understandings of salvation as a participatory undertaking were shaped by distinctively English ways of thinking about human development, human morality, and the purpose (or final destiny) of human life itself. Those who joined the great English experiment of transatlantic colonization, beginning in the sixteenth and seventeenth centuries, embraced an ideology of progress that remains a hallmark of American culture today. As a clash of civilizations played out in North America, this same ideology led English colonists, over time, to all but abandon their stated aim of Indian evangelization, to embrace an economic system predicated on the labor of enslaved Africans and their descendants, and to construct a hierarchical and racialized caste system in which they came to conceive of themselves as "white."

These ancient ways of thinking about ultimate aims continue to fuel powerful American aspirations of "progress" on many fronts. They also continue to shape the racial attitudes of white Americans today, and they remain powerfully present in the institutionalized racism that still characterizes American public life.

The Doctrine of Salvation

As did their counterparts in Europe, English people living in the early modern era inherited from their medieval forebears the understanding that God had created an intrinsically hierarchical world. In this way of thinking, a great "chain of being" governed all manner of life, beginning with God and descending through angels, humans, animals, plants, and minerals. Within each of these categories of beings, likewise, there existed a naturally ordered system of stages or "ranks." The work of constructing classifications of things within this vast system occupied some of the early modern era's greatest minds. It also inspired the realm of study called "natural history" that became a hallmark of the European Renaissance.

Early English Protestants agreed with their European contemporaries that human beings were unique in the chain of being in that they spanned the spiritual and physical worlds.[2] As they found the human condition described in one of their most beloved psalms:

> O Lord, our Lord, . . . When I consider thy heavens, the work of thy fingers, the moon and the stars, which thou hast ordained; What is man, that thou art mindful of him? and the son of man, that thou visitest him? For thou hast made him a little lower than the angels, and hast crowned him with glory and honour. (Psalm 8:3–6, KJV)

Humans were subject to all the vicissitudes of their animal nature, and yet they were also capable of transcending this nature. How best to do so dominated debates within English Protestantism for centuries. Most came to think of the spiritual life as a struggle in this life to prepare for eternal salvation in the next. English Protestants had a simple way of describing this struggle: they called it progress.

The Church of England's views on this matter were clearly articulated by the Anglican cleric Jeremy Taylor. Born in 1613, educated at All Souls College, Oxford, and a protégé of William Laud, Archbishop of Canterbury, Taylor served as chaplain in the Royal Army and became the personal chaplain to King Charles I. After Charles was executed—"martyred," his loyal followers insisted—on January 30, 1649, Taylor sought to extract the "means and instruments of obtaining every virtue" from the examples of those, like Charles, who followed faithfully in Jesus's footsteps. This quest resulted in the publication of his celebrated twin volumes, *The Rules and Exercises of Holy Living* (1650) and *The Rules and Exercises of Holy Dying* (1651). In Taylor's view, God had intended for human life to be "long and happy, without sickness, sorrow or infelicity," but because of Adam's fall, "man . . . fell from that state to a contrary." Taylor believed that the essence of human life was therefore a preparation to die and that the truly faithful would pursue holiness, such that by the time they died they would be spiritually equipped to share life with God for eternity.[3] Sometimes printed separately and often combined under the same cover, Taylor's *Holy Living* and *Holy Dying* went through twenty-five London editions by 1739 and were widely circulated in Anglican circles on both sides of the Atlantic.[4]

If Jeremy Taylor set the template for the spiritual journey of the Anglican faithful, John Bunyan did the same for dissenting Protestants. Born in 1628, Bunyan enlisted in the Parliamentary Army at the age of sixteen, during the height of the English Civil War (1642–51). After three years of military service Bunyan embraced the culture of English "nonconformity," became notorious for his passionate preaching of dissent, and was imprisoned multiple times across fifteen years for violating the Conventicle Act, the 1664 Act of Parliament forbidding "conventicles," or religious gatherings, outside the auspices of the Church of England. While in prison, Bunyan wrote a theological tract, *Grace Abounding to the Chief of Sinners*, and *The Pilgrim's Progress*, for which he would become most well-known. Formally entitled *The Pilgrim's Progress from this World to That which is to Come*, Bunyan's epic allegory tells the story of an ordinary man named Christian, who—while confronting unimaginable trials and tribulations—eventually reaches his destination, the Celestial City of God. In transit, Christian meets up with other sojourners with names like "Faithful" and "Hopeful," who accompany him through perilous landscapes with names like "Hill Difficulty" and the "Slough of Despond."[5]

With its first part published in London in 1678, and its second part the next year, *Pilgrim's Progress* met with such widespread acclaim that it ran through more than twenty-five editions in its first quarter century of publication, and it remained among the most widely printed books in the English language straight through to the middle of the nineteenth century.[6]

From the most loyal Anglican to the most fervent Puritan, then, English Protestants at every point along the spectrum of dissent understood the life of faith to be analogous to a journey or better yet a climb up the rungs of a ladder at the top of which would be found spiritual deliverance. They understood this ladder to be singular, which is to say that it applied to all human beings, and so they understood that English colonial projects should naturally include the twin projects of English civilization and Protestant evangelization.

Among the earliest champions of the English colonial enterprise in North America was the lawyer Richard Hakluyt's nephew, an Anglican priest of the same name who spent decades at his writing desk in London compiling, editing, and disseminating the accounts of early explorers. In *The Principal Navigations of the English*, a three-volume work published between 1598 and 1600, the younger Richard Hakluyt romanticized English explorers across the ages, tracing their spiritual lineage backward and forward in time.[7] Hakluyt saw a direct line between the explorers of his day—men like Sir Francis Drake and Sir Walter Raleigh—and King Arthur, the early medieval monarch of the late fifth and early sixth centuries. Arthur had conquered Norway, Iceland, Greenland, and other northern territories where the people were, according to Hakluyt, "wild and savage, and had not in them the love of God nor of their neighbors." Hakluyt saw these efforts, in turn, as a continuation of the process by which Roman conquerors had first brought the Christian gospel to Britain in the fourth and fifth centuries. At the time, the residents of the British

Isles—the ancient peoples called Picts—were also "wild and savage," Hakluyt explained, and yet the Romans had introduced them to Christianity and brought them to civilization.

Generations of English Protestants would embrace Hakluyt's view that the English project of colonizing North America was an entirely logical extension of this unilinear historic process. They would disagree over who was best suited to become for the natives of North America what Arthur had been for the peoples of Scandinavia and what the Romans had been for the Picts. Some thought the chief evangelists should be missionaries sent by the bishops of the Church of England, while others thought the task would best be carried out by Puritan colonists seeking to remove themselves from the influence of Anglican authorities. Regardless, English Protestants who set their sights on North America agreed with Hakluyt's essential conclusion: it was incumbent on the English to "cover the naked miserie" of the peoples on the far sides of the Atlantic, to bring them out of the wilderness and into the state of civilization, and to set their feet on the path to salvation.[8] The same could be said of the peoples of the darkest continent, Africa. After all, this was what progress looked like.

The Hardening of American Slavery

The first generations of English Protestants to colonize North America did not imagine that their enterprises would come to depend on slave labor. In fact, many fancied that their ventures would serve as a rebuke of the Spanish and Portuguese, whose abuses in trafficking African slaves they saw as expressions of Catholic tyranny. These abuses had been vividly chronicled by the Spanish priest Bartolome de las Casas, whose reports were translated and distributed widely throughout Europe. Las Casas's reports provoked widespread debate over whether the Native peoples of Africa and the Americas had souls, which is to say whether they had the capacity to divine the One True God and could therefore be seen as falling within the evangelical purview of conquering European powers.[9] The intrinsic backwardness of these peoples seemed obvious to all Europeans, but by what could this backwardness be explained and by what means—if any—could it be remedied? Where did the peoples of these "newly discovered" lands presently sit in the great Chain of Being, and how far could they be expected to advance? As they entered the colonial competition for North America, the English immediately confronted these fundamental questions.

Most early champions of English colonization found ample reason for optimism. Richard Hakluyt, for instance, scoured his sources and concluded—as summarized by Peter Mancall—that because "the natives possessed a set of religious beliefs, however barbarous," they were legitimate candidates for evangelization. Referencing the atrocities recounted by Las Casas, Hakluyt asserted that surely peoples formerly subject to Catholic colonizers could "easily be induced to live subject to the gentle government of the English."[10]

Their professed revulsion at the slave-trading practices of the Spanish and Portuguese did not mean early English Protestants found slavery intolerable in and of itself. Consistent with their conceptions of a natural human hierarchy, the English understood that a hereditary monarchy, an extensive system of "peerage," and a vast pool of unranked people ("commoners") had been divinely ordained. They also understood that more common kinds of labor were naturally spread along a spectrum of servile relationships. "Servant" and "service" were the umbrella terms covering the entire range, but the labels "tenant," "bond servant," "indentured servant," and "apprentice" each suggested a different kind of relationship that obligated servants to their masters.[11] The notion of slavery fit comfortably at the bottom of this hierarchical view, so much so that the venerated English churchman Thomas More included the institution in his vision of *Utopia*, first published in 1516.

English speakers on both sides of the Atlantic continued to celebrate More's vision straight through the eighteenth century, a
clear tell that the idea of a society without some form of slavery
remained quite literally beyond their imagination.[12]

Neither did their acceptance of slavery set early English
Protestants apart in what today's historians call "the Atlantic
World," in which the peoples of four continents—Europe,
Africa, and North and South America—were increasingly
connected by advances in maritime technology. Many native
tribes in the Americas enslaved captives as a common practice
of warfare. The peoples of West Africa were accustomed to
trafficking enemy captives as slaves, both to each other and
to European traders. Different forms of human captivity and
bondage were practiced in every corner of Europe. As advances
in maritime technology continued to propel transatlantic
commerce across the sixteenth and seventeenth centuries,
it was simply taken for granted in all corners of the Atlantic
world that enslavement was a natural consequence of being
taken captive in war. But what this meant varied greatly from
one context to the next. There was not one single system of
slavery, but rather many dynamic systems of slavery, each of
which evolved across time.[13]

In his 1975 classic, *American Slavery, American Freedom*,
Edmund Morgan chronicled how English colonists in North
America developed a racialized system of "chattel slavery,"
centered in the colony of Virginia. English colonists established
the first permanent settlement near present-day Williamsburg
in 1607, honoring the English King by naming it Jamestown.
Relations with Native peoples of the Chesapeake fell apart even
more quickly in Virginia than they would a few decades later
in New England. Extreme famine led to the early humiliation
of the Jamestown colonists having to depend on Indian benev-
olence. Widespread hostilities ensued when the Indians proved
unwilling to conform to the code of conduct the colonists

called the "Lawes Divine, Morall, and Martial." In response to an Indian massacre in March 1622, the English in Virginia embarked on a campaign of Indian decimation they would sustain for generations.[14]

The discovery that Virginia's soil made tobacco a rewarding cash crop, meanwhile, led Virginia's elites to seek the continued acquisition of land and the continual replenishment of the colonial labor force. Indian lands could be obtained by force, but with Virginia's natives proving poor candidates for conscription, Virginia's leaders quickly pivoted to encourage the immigration of indentured English servants for the cultivation of tobacco. This system afforded Virginia tobacco planters extraordinary control over their laborers, so much so that, in Morgan's estimation, they began to "treat men as things."[15]

Eventually, Virginian elites could wring only so much labor out of this system of indenture, and so they began to look for another model of plantation development. They found one in the West Indies, where English planters had responded to stunning rates of mortality by embracing a plantation economy predicated on brutal practices of forced labor and the continual arrival of new African slaves.[16] By the end of the seventeenth century, Virginia's elites had committed themselves almost entirely to an economy predicated on African slave labor.[17] Where earlier generations of Virginians had been open to including the people they called "Negroes" as full members of their communities through baptism, in 1662 the colony's leaders revised their statutes, unlinking baptism and emancipation. Simultaneously, they codified the Roman principle of *partus sequitur ventrum*, meaning that the offspring inherited the status of their mothers.[18] African slaves in Virginia—and soon enough in almost all the English colonies of North America—became "chattel," an old English word derived from the same root as the word "cattle." Their condition of lifelong servitude would be passed down through the generations.

Historians of early America today understand that all this happened before today's racial categories were fully developed.[19] And it would not be until the nineteenth century that full-blown theories of racial difference would be justified in terms of biological science.[20] But the template for white American racism was being set as early as the seventeenth century. When Indians and Africans were merely "heathen," they fell within the ranks of human and as such were seen as eligible both for freedom in this life and for salvation in the next. But the English in North America increasingly doubted the humanity of people their ancestors had considered candidates for civilization and evangelization. In the estimation of the English, the "savage" Indians and the "brutish" Negroes had fallen from within the ranking of humans, to a new category that fell short—no one knew exactly how far short—of humanity.[21] The former were hard to tame and adept in the ways of surviving the North American wilderness. But the latter, the African slaves and their descendants, had nowhere to flee. They could be broken, as could other creatures of "bestial" nature.

The spread of slavery in places like Virginia drew all of England's North American colonies even more deeply into the "triangle trade" that tied places as far-flung as Boston, Amsterdam, Senegal, and Barbados into a web of mutual interdependence.[22] Northern colonists depended on southern tobacco plantations and Caribbean sugar plantations for the export of their grain, livestock, and forest products, even as they professed to look down on the practice of slaveholding. As Woody Holton has observed, "In the vitally important economic sphere they, too, were slave societies."[23] Across the eighteenth century, the population of the English colonies in North America effectively doubled each generation—from some 300,000 at the start of the century to almost four million when the US Constitution was signed in 1787.[24] This dramatic growth resulted partly from increased rates of natural birth, partly from improved living conditions and increased longevity especially in the northern colonies, and partly from new levels of immigration from the British Isles and other European nations. An explosion in the traffic of African slaves, however, played an indispensable role. At least a quarter of a million Africans were forcibly trafficked to the English colonies on the mainland of North America between 1700 and 1775. At the onset of the American Revolution, Black slaves constituted 40 percent of Virginia's population and 60 percent of South Carolina's.[25]

Historians today understand more fully than ever how the enslaved were able to exercise different kinds of power and different degrees of resistance within this system. Scholars like Walter Johnson have shown how many slaves were able to create leverage within the complex and "interpenetrated" relations of slaves and slave-sellers, adjusting their value through cooperation or noncooperation, for instance, to secure certain outcomes. Similarly, not all slaves were without power in their relationships with their owners, and not all slave families were treated equally, even within the same household or plantation. In her majestic study of Thomas Jefferson's relationship with *The Hemingses of Monticello*, Annette Gordon-Reed has shown how some enslaved women—while lacking the freedom that would allow for true consent—were nonetheless able to work their "unions with white men who were their legal masters . . . to their advantage and to the advantages of their children and later descendants." Some enslaved men, too, attained "some degree of freedom within [their] enslaved status." As Gordon-Reed sums things up: "The profanity of slavery does not define the entirety of the lives of enslaved people," and historians have "long since moved beyond the notion that slave owners were deity-like in their omnipotence and that slaves really were actual chattel, like pieces of furniture lacking consciences and will."[26]

All this notwithstanding, at the root of the American system lay the "chattel principle," which enabled slave-sellers and slave-owners to subject their slaves to perpetual fear. In part this fear was physical, grounded in the continual hardening of slave labor discipline across the eighteenth century. As Morgan summarized, "In order to get work out of men and women who had nothing to gain but absence of pain, you had to be willing to beat, maim, and kill. And society had to be ready to back you even to the point of footing the bill for the property you killed."[27] According to Johnson, however, the deepest fear resulted from the threat of being separated from family members, a threat often realized and even more often conjured. As conditions continued to worsen through the middle decades of the eighteenth century, enslaved Blacks resorted more frequently to outright rebellion, ratcheting the tension with their owners.[28]

Through it all, until the mid-eighteenth century, virtually all devout Protestants on both sides of the Atlantic simply took for granted that slavery was a fixed part of the North American enterprise. This includes even those Protestants in whom some historians see the early stirrings of abolitionist sentiment, men like Samuel Davies. Commissioned in 1747 by the New-Castle Presbytery of neighboring Delaware to establish a network of preaching points in Virginia, Davies began to include African and African American slaves in his services of worship in the early 1750s. Arguing that true faith was best cultivated by both hearing and reading the Word, he even secured permission from several slaveowners to teach their slaves to read and to admit them for formal membership in his Presbyterian congregations. In 1754, Davies summarized his recent success as having been "chiefly among the extremes of Gentlemen and Negroes. Indeed, God has been remarkably working among the latter. I have baptized about 150 adults; and at the last sacramental solemnity, I had the pleasure of seeing the table graced with about 60 black faces."[29] And in a 1757 sermon, entitled *The Duty of Christians to Propagate their Religion among Heathens*, Davies addressed "the Masters of Negroes in Virginia," commending that "sundry of you not only consent that your Negroes should receive instruction from me, but also zealously concur with me, and make conscience of your own duty to them, in this respect." Davies's rationale for this was clear enough, as he explained in opening the sermon:

> A creature formed for immortality, and that must be happy or miserable through an everlasting duration, is certainly a being of vast importance, however mean and insignificant he may be in other respects. His immortality gives him a kind of infinite value. Let him be white or black, bond or free, a native or a foreigner, it is of no moment in this view: he is to live forever, to be forever happy, or forever miserable! Happy or miserable in the highest degree! This places him upon a kind of equality with Kings and Princes; nay, with Angels and Arch-Angels . . .

Appealing to the paternalistic instincts of Virginia's slave-owners, Davies concluded by challenging them to consider "How vast, how awful the trust! To be instrumental to render such a being happy, through its immortal duration! To 'SAVE A SOUL FROM DEATH'. . . . How benevolent, how noble an exploit, how glorious a salvation is this!"[30] Davies's focus on the eternal dimension of salvation was telling—at no time in his career did he call for the abolition of slavery, and he justified his own slaveholding by the benevolent character of his ownership.[31]

The notion that slavery could be reconciled readily with the promises of Christianity was also championed by George Whitefield, the itinerant Anglican revivalist who would achieve monumental fame on both sides of the Atlantic across the middle decades of the eighteenth century. Born in

Gloucester, England, in 1714, George Whitefield "came up" to Oxford University in 1735, a prodigious step-up for the son of innkeepers. At Oxford, he fell in with the brothers John and Charles Wesley, leaders of a small group devoted to fomenting spiritual renewal within the Church of England. Mocked by their peers for their fanaticism, the young men took names intended as insults and embraced them as badges of honor— the "Holy Club," for their pietism, and "Methodists," for their rigorous discipline.[32] The Wesley brothers and George Whitefield began their work as Anglican priests by traveling to the English colony of Georgia as missionaries for the Society for the Propagation of the Gospel (SPG), the Church of England's initiative designed to revitalize the American church.[33] George Whitefield's preaching met with great enthusiasm during his missionary sojourn. When he returned to America in the late fall of 1739, Whitefield was embraced as a celebrity, preaching in the open air to enormous gatherings that included Blacks and whites, men and women, European colonists and Native Americans.[34]

Whitefield invited controversy by preaching outdoors (and often uninvited) in Anglican parishes throughout North America. His defenders asserted he was preaching nothing but Jeremy Taylor's orthodox views of holiness, instructing his listeners that "If they could be carry'd up into that blessed Place in an unregenerate State, it would be an Hell to them; their Souls not being made holy here, they could not endure the Holiness there."[35] Whitefield saw no contradiction between holiness and slave-owning, however. As he labored to stand up an Orphan House in Bethesda, Georgia, beginning in the 1740s, he advocated forcefully for the legalization of slavery in the new colony. Already the owner of slaves in South Carolina—where supporters had donated slaveholding farms to support his ministry—Whitefield was challenged by some of his contemporaries for his outspoken support of the institution.

As he explained to his fellow Methodist John Wesley in 1751, he found slavery to be justified on biblical, economic, racial, and climatic grounds.

> As to the lawfulness of keeping slaves, I have no doubt, since I hear of some that were bought with Abraham's money [Genesis 21:12], and some that were born in his house [Genesis 17:23]. I, also, cannot help thinking, that some of those servants mentioned by the apostles, in their epistles, were or had been slaves [e.g., Onesimus]. It is plain that the Gibeonites were doomed to perpetual slavery [Joshua 9:26–27]; and, though liberty is a sweet thing to such as are born free, yet to those who never knew the sweets of it, slavery perhaps may not be so irksome. However this be, it is plain that hot countries cannot be cultivated without negroes.

Whitefield was unapologetic. "What a flourishing country might Georgia have been," he wrote to Wesley, "had the use of slavery been permitted years ago!"[36]

Not all slaveholders in North America shared Whitefield's lack of moral compunction, but almost all, as good English Protestants, embraced the scriptures as a way of reconciling themselves to the practice. When his friend Robert Pleasant gifted him a copy of the Quaker Anthony Benezet's antislavery tract in 1773, the notoriously devout Patrick Henry responded with thanks, commending the Quakers "for their noble Effort to abolish Slavery" while at the same time exclaiming: "It is not a little surprising that Christianity, whose chief excellence consists in softening the human heart, in cherishing & improving its finer Feelings, should encourage a Practice so totally repugnant to the first Impression of right & wrong."[37]

Advancing the White Race

Biblical interpretation was not the only justification of slaveholding in revolutionary circles. Across the middle decades of the century, as the English colonies in North America grew ever more connected to one another, their leaders increasingly began to think of themselves as "white." This new racialized self-understanding was forged in the context of increasingly diverse colonial populations, which saw large streams of immigration from other parts of the British Isles and Europe, in addition to the explosive growth of African slaves and their descendants.[38] Lacking even rudimentary understandings of human biology, colonial leaders struggled to make sense of the diversity in burgeoning cities like Boston, New York, and Philadelphia in the only way they knew how—by attempting to construct categories that would allow them to place the many peoples that surrounded them within the Great Chain of Being.

Most proximately, they focused on the superficial characteristics of physical features, beginning with the colors of human skin, which they took as signs of deep fundamental differences. Thomas Jefferson shared these views with the public in his *Notes on the State of Virginia*, which were published in 1787.[39] In these Notes, Jefferson wrote approvingly of "colonization," the proposal to resettle Africans from America in a distant land. He would maintain this view to the end of his life, at root because he feared that white prejudices and Black resentments made a future race war almost inevitable.[40] To these "political" obstacles to a peaceful reconciliation between the races in America, however, Jefferson added a host of others based on "the real distinctions which nature has made."

Jefferson began with the most striking distinction of color, asking, "Is it not the foundation of a greater or less share of beauty in the two races?" After expounding on additional "physical distinctions proving a difference of race," he turned to matters of morality. Allowing that Blacks are "at least as brave, and more adventuresome" than whites, he cautioned, "But this may perhaps proceed from a want of forethought, which prevents their seeing a danger till it be present." In general, he observed, "their existence appears to participate more of sensation than reflection." And then matters intellectual:

> Comparing them by their faculties of memory, reason, and imagination, it appears to me, that in memory they are equal to the whites; in reason much inferior, as I think one could scarcely be found capable of tracing and comprehending the investigations of Euclid; and that in imagination they are dull, tasteless, and anomalous.

Granting allowances "for the difference of condition, of education, of conversation, of the sphere in which they move," Jefferson contrasted them with Indians, who can "astonish you with strokes of the most sublime oratory; such as prove their reason and sentiment strong, their imagination glowing and elevated. . . . But never yet could I find that a black had uttered a thought above the level of plain narration." Ranking the American poet Phyllis Wheatley and the Black British abolitionist Ignatius Sancho at the "bottom of the column" of writers in his day, he wrote of the latter: "This criticism supposes the letters published under his name to be genuine, and to have received amendment from no other hand; points which would not be of easy investigation."

But for Jefferson the clearest indication of Black inferiority was the "improvement" in both "body and mind" that was made manifest "in the first instance of their mixture with the whites." This "has been observed by every one," he asserted, "and proves that their inferiority is not the effect merely of their condition of life." Jefferson's views were widespread among Virginia's elites, who were perpetually attempting to quantify the bloodlines of their mixed-race slaves. These attempts were sustained across generations, of course, because so too was the practice that Jefferson would adopt in 1789, the practice of fathering children with one of his own slaves, Sally Hemings. Sally Hemings was in fact the half-sister of Jefferson's wife, Martha, owing to the fact that she was the child of Martha's father, John Wayles, and one of his slaves, Elizabeth Hemings. According to family legend, Martha Jefferson secured a promise from Thomas never to remarry before she died at age thirty-four in 1784. Five years later, Sally, then fourteen, traveled to Paris to accompany her brothers, James and Robert, in their service to Jefferson while he was the US ambassador to France. In Paris—apparently after Sally had turned sixteen—Jefferson, then forty-six, initiated the relationship that over thirty years produced six children.[41]

Thomas Jefferson worked assiduously to keep his relationship with Sally Hemings hidden from public view, and if he ever mentioned her in his private correspondence, he—or perhaps his descendants—culled such mention from his papers. Whatever "interior" sense he made of this relationship, Jefferson also considered it within another frame of meaning in which he sustained a lifelong interest—the frame that he called "natural history."

Jefferson spent George Washington's second presidential term (1793–97) almost entirely at his Monticello plantation. From there he sustained a prolific correspondence with Washington and other Virginia plantation owners. He included in this correspondence regular updates on his progress in farming Monticello, including his determination to fill its farmlands with Spanish "Merino" sheep. Jefferson valued the Merino because he observed them both to produce the finest wool and to improve the productivity of the lands they grazed and fertilized.[42] In 1795, after being gifted a Merino ram by his friend Richard Morris, Jefferson gave the ram free rein over his pastures, continually breeding the ram's offspring with his stock of "common sheep." By the year 1810 he believed his entire flock had now become "as pure as the original," as he demonstrated with a mathematical formula in a letter to William Thornton.[43] That same year he explained to another of his favorite correspondents, James Madison, a method by which they could share the wealth with their fellow Virginians, by giving "all the full blooded males we can raise to the different counties of our state, one to each, as fast as we can furnish them." Jefferson's letter to Madison included some simple calculations to estimate how fast "our whole state may thus, from this small stock . . . be filled in a very few years, with this valuable race."[44]

Five years later Jefferson shared similar calculations with his friend Francis Gray, but this time in response to Gray's query as to "what constituted a mulatto by our law?" Where Jefferson had previously told Gray that the answer to the question was "4 crossings with the whites," he wrote now with an update: "1/4 of negro blood, mixed with any portion of white, constitutes the mulatto." Jefferson allowed that the law was imprecise, because "the blood of each parent . . . may be made up of a variety of fractional mixtures," rendering the matter "a Mathematical problem of the same class with those on the mixtures of different liquors or different metals." He then followed with an extended "Algebraical notation" to make the matter "most convenient & intelligible," a notation much like the one he employed in his correspondence about Merino sheep. He then elaborated: "it is understood in Natural history that a 4th cross of one race of animals with another gives an issue equivalent for all sensible purposes to the original blood." He illustrated with this example: "thus a Merino ram being crossed 1st with a country ewe, 2dly with this daughter, 3dly with this grandaughter, and 4thly with the great grandaughter, the last issue is deemed pure Merino, having in fact but 1/16 of the country blood." Therefore, he concluded: "our Canon considers 2 crosses with the pure white, and a 3d with any degree of mixture, however small, as clearing the issue of the negro blood." He then cautioned Gray to remember that "this does not reestablish freedom, which depends on the condition of the mother," citing "the principle of the civil law, partus sequitur ventrem." But, he concluded, if such a person were to "be emancipated, he becomes a free white man, and a citizen of the US."[45] Jefferson underlined the key word, "white."

It is impossible to imagine Thomas Jefferson conducting this correspondence without considering its implications for his own children by Sally Hemings. After all, in the terms that prevailed in colonial Virginia, Sally's mother, Elizabeth, was "mulatto," having been born to an African woman and her slaveowner, John Hemings. Sally was therefore "quadroon" (or "one-quarter negro"), because she was the daughter of Elizabeth and her white owner, John Wayles (the father of Martha Wayles, who became Jefferson's wife). This meant that Sally's children by Jefferson were "octoroon," or "one-eighth negro," which is to say even further along the path that Jefferson considered identical to the "natural" path he was pursuing in his attempts to improve his stock of sheep. Although they lacked the language of eugenics that would arise in the United States and elsewhere in the nineteenth and twentieth centuries, early Virginian slaveowners like John Hemings, John Wayles, and Thomas Jefferson did not lack the concept that would enable its spread. Through their relationships with their enslaved Black women, they understood themselves to be "clearing the issue of negro blood" and advancing the superior white race.

Across his remaining four decades of life, Thomas Jefferson came to rue the frankness with which he had shared his thoughts on race in his *Notes on the State of Virginia*. Why did he choose to publish views that by his own admission to a friend were "the result of personal observation on the limited sphere of my own State," where, he admitted, conditions for the development of Blacks were "not favorable"?[46] Why did he do so even though—as he later explained to another correspondent—he feared that other Virginians might use them to undermine his stated objectives, one of which was "the emancipation of their slaves"?[47] He explained himself by pointing to the importance of advancing human knowledge. "To our reproach," he explained, "it must be said, that though for a century and a half we have had under our eyes the races of black and of red men, they have never yet been viewed by us as subjects of natural history."[48] Like generations of English Protestants before him, and like others of his generation and beyond, the enlightened Jefferson could not resist attempting to draw fine distinctions between creatures he understood to reside somewhere within the Great Chain of Being.

To say that white English Protestants in revolutionary America took slavery for granted is not to say that they accepted it uniformly. Just as the conditions of slavery and the practices of slave-owning varied across time and place, so did people's views of the practice. It is easy now to cherry-pick quotations from the slave-owning founders as a means of demonstrating their moral abhorrence at the institution. Already in his 1773 letter to Anthony Benezet, Patrick Henry wrote, "I believe a time will come when an opportunity will be offered to abolish this lamentable Evil." In 1786, George Washington wrote of slavery, "there is not a man living who wishes more sincerely than I do, to see a plan adopted for the abolition of it." In 1787 James Madison called slavery "the most oppressive dominion ever exercised by man over man."[49] In his 1787 *Notes*, Thomas Jefferson had asserted that "The spirit of the master is abating, that of the slave rising from the dust, his condition mollifying, the way I hope preparing, under the auspices of heaven, for a total emancipation."[50]

But these expressed hopes compelled none of the men who wrote them to pursue with any seriousness the emancipation of their own slaves. George Washington expressed in his will the desire that some of his slaves—those "which I hold in [my] *own right*"—shall be freed. But instead of doing so directly, he bequeathed them to his wife, Martha, whose family owned the rights to most of the Mount Vernon slaves, knowing that the intermarriages and economic relations of the plantation would render his expressed desire a moot point.[51] James Madison left the thirty-six slaves he owned to his wife, Dolly, who sold some and bequeathed the remainder to her son. Jefferson had reluctantly freed James Hemings in 1796 and in his will freed five additional men from the Hemings family—perhaps fulfilling a promise to Sally.[52] But despite his lifelong wrestling with the issue, and despite his constant expression of moral abhorrence at the nature of the relations that slavery inspired between Blacks and whites, he left the remaining of Monticello's 130 slaves to his heirs, most of whom were sold off to retire family debt.[53]

However they blended the mix of English Protestantism and Enlightenment philosophy that comprised their religious views, the slaveowners who played such a decisive role in the founding of the United States had fully reconciled themselves to what Edmund Morgan described as "the central paradox of American history"—the simultaneous growth of freedom for some and growth of slavery for others.[54] Some followed in the footsteps of Samuel Davies and George Whitefield— they conceived of America's enslaved Negroes as qualified for eternal salvation, but with this aim in mind they fixed them permanently as slaves in this life, at the very bottom rung in the rank of servants. Others, like Thomas Jefferson, constructed altogether new categories for their Black chattel, categories that capped their potential for progress just short of the human species. Whatever their interior struggles with the society they and their forebears had created, in the eyes of the men who founded the United States, their Black slaves were rightly consigned to be property in this life. And it could be left to God to sort out their eternal fates.

Progress and White Racism

English colonists arriving in North America across the seventeenth and eighteenth centuries brought with them an early

English Protestant understanding of "progress," grounded in a unilinear conception of human development, particular understandings of social hierarchy and servanthood, and the conviction that the truly faithful were called to "work out their salvation." From these ideological roots sprung one of the most successful colonial enterprises in the history of humankind. Early Americans grounded in this tradition developed noble cultural traits with which people around the world associate the United States even still today—proud, principled, aspirational, forward-looking.

But a Christian heresy that is equally characteristic of American culture—the heresy of white supremacy—springs from these same ideological roots. As Native peoples continued to contest the English occupation of North America, more and more colonists concluded that the Indians were not "heathen," but "savage," and therefore unsuited to civilization. So, the colonists accelerated their territorial expansion, casting the "red" Indians further into the wilderness. Since the Indians were not "settled," and since one patch of wilderness was much like any other, what did it matter if they were forced off their current land? And as trafficked Africans and their descendants resisted the docility and submission that their slaveholders demanded, more and more English colonists attributed their conduct to a "bestial" nature, casting their "Negroe" slaves as chattel. Some considered "Black" slaves as fully human, and therefore as candidates for eternal salvation, but this did not alter their status in this life—after all, the Bible clearly sanctioned slavery. Others, as the Belgian anthropologist van den Berghe sums things up, reconciled their "democratic, egalitarian and libertarian ideals . . . with slavery and genocide by restricting the definition of humanity to whites."[55]

American white racism combines a caste system characterized by hierarchical thinking—what Edmund Morgan long ago described as "a generalized English contempt for those of low rank"—and an architecture of racial categories first developed by English colonists.[56] Born originally from English bewilderment at the demographic diversity of colonial North America, this white American racism vastly outweighed emerging abolitionist sentiments in the Continental Congresses, and in the Constitutional Conventions, where delegates settled on the assessment that each of the new nation's Negroes constituted three-fifths of a man in apportioning representation among the states. Slaveholding Virginians held the office of president for thirty-two of the office's first thirty-six years, and down through to the middle of the twentieth century almost every American president expressed openly Thomas Jefferson's toxic mix of hierarchical thinking and racial categorization. Donald Trump carried this banner proudly into the twenty-first century, embracing the discourse of white racism unabashedly in his successful 2016 presidential campaign.[57]

A charitable rendering of our nation's founding sees within it the seeds of slavery's demise. In this rendering from the Heritage Foundation, for instance:

> the American Revolution introduced natural rights principles of liberty and equality that eroded the institution of slavery in the new republic. After 1776, several northern states, some of which had a considerable percentage of slaves, either freed their slaves outright or started gradual emancipation schemes. In 1782, Virginia allowed slave owners to manumit (voluntarily emancipate) their slaves, and thousands were freed. In 1787, Congress passed the Northwest Ordinance, which banned slavery in the new states north of the Ohio River that were created out of the Northwest Territory.[58]

But renderings like this bury the truth that the United States was founded on more than the high-minded ideals articulated in its founding documents. It was also born from an intercolonial movement that simply assumed the "white race" to be superior to others and likewise assumed that "American" equaled "white." This ethnonationalist identity developed in parallel to an emerging sense of "continental" destiny, as we saw in the last chapter, and to a new and generic Protestant vernacular, as we will see in the next. In this way the nascent national identity of the United States was culturally, racially, and religiously grounded.

White Americans today are still powerfully shaped by this ideology of white racism, a Christian heresy. This heresy has become central to the faith of some. According to Philip Gorski and Samuel Perry, polling shows that "For many White Americans, Christianity is more of an ethnic culture and identity than a set of spiritual beliefs. It means 'White people like us.'"[59] Surprisingly, this ideology does not require a virulent hate of nonwhite persons, however, nor even a deep-rooted conviction of their basic inferiority. In his 1773 letter to Anthony Benezet, Patrick Henry expressed astonishment at his own predicament as if it were inescapable: "Would any one believe that I am Master of Slaves of my own purchase!" He then confessed: "I am drawn along by [the] general inconvenience of living without them, I will not, I cannot justify it. However culpable my Conduct, I will so far pay my devoir [from the French for "debt"] to Virtue, as to own the excellence & rectitude of her Precepts, & to lament my want of conforming to them."[60] Henry's *mea culpa* reflects Gordon-Reed's conclusion that for some white supremacists "ruthless self-interest, not sincere belief, is the signature feature of the doctrine."[61] None of us who are white and American and Christian today own slaves, but we all live perpetually subject to the spiritual temptation that Henry articulated so concisely and that Jefferson embodied so completely.

While writing this book I attended a conference in central San Diego hosted by the local diocese of the Episcopal Church, the church which separated from the Church of England in the aftermath of the American Revolution, the church to which Thomas Jefferson belonged. The keynote speaker was Bishop Michael Curry, the twenty-seventh presiding bishop and primate of the Episcopal Church. An African American descended from slaves in North Carolina on both sides of his family, Bishop Curry spoke eloquently on the conference theme, which was the intersection of the Christian gospel and social justice. I felt very much at home in the audience, filled with organizers and champions and supporters of social justice like me. The audience was overwhelmingly white.

During a break in the program, I stepped out of the large dining room to go to the bathroom. In the hall I came across the waitstaff, who were on a break after serving the main course. Some three dozen workers were chatting amiably in small clusters, almost all in Spanish. Finally, one man shouted, "Ahora sí, amigos, el postre, el postre!" (Now's the time, friends, dessert, dessert!) As I watched the waiters scatter to their serving stations, it became clear to me that every single one of them was brown skinned. As it is in every major city in the United States, the service sector of San Diego's economy is utterly dependent on the low-wage labor of people of color. Here in my part of the world, most brown-skinned workers are people of Mexican descent. The supervisor, also brown skinned, simply took for granted that Spanish was the right language to call his team back to work.

Having been born and raised here, I understand how San Diego's economy is organized. Unable to afford the housing prices in San Diego, most of the city's low-wage workers now live at a lengthy commute from their jobs. Some commute for several hours from California's inland communities, where the costs of housing are cheaper. Others—numbering some 150,000—live in Tijuana and wait hours in line each morning to cross the border to come to work. Almost all these cross-border workers are US citizens of Mexican ancestry who can't afford to live in San Diego's downtown, or in the city's wealthy, predominantly white, northern neighborhoods where they work.

I stopped for a moment to wonder what a neutral, outside observer might make of this elaborate choreography. Of course, they would not see the horrors of early American chattel slavery. I am not equating current arrangements with what John Adams long ago called "an evil of colossal magnitude."[62] But were their vantage sufficiently far removed—I imagined a distant, bird's-eye view—my imaginary neutral observer would not be able to diagnose the mechanisms by which this labor market was organized. Looking from above on the gathering I attended that night in central San Diego, what they would see is a society profoundly organized around "upstairs/downstairs" dynamics and skin color. Apart from the racial–ethnic composition of the workforce, I suspect things would not be much different in most such gatherings across the United States.

Later I tried to imagine that this neutral, outside observer was not far removed geographically, but far removed into the future. I imagined this observer traveling back in time, and zooming in even further, so far that they could get a close look at me, sitting comfortably at my table, enjoying a fine meal and glass of wine. Is it possible that this observer from the future might find my passive acceptance of this social arrangement as baffling—or repulsive, even—as I find Thomas Jefferson's speculative resignation at the plight of his enslaved offspring?

CHAPTER 4

Truth
Innovation and Propaganda

The way early English Protestants thought about it, the Bible contained the greatest truth of all, the good news—or "gospel"—of what God had done for humankind in the birth, life, death, and resurrection of Jesus Christ. As Jesus himself made clear: "I am the way, the truth, and the life: no man cometh unto the Father, but by me" (John 14:6, KJV). In fact, the most devout Protestants considered the Bible a singular and authoritative source of fundamental truths about all manner of things, from the transcendental to the mundane. Living centuries before the emergence of historical-critical methods of interpreting Scripture, they did not seek to discover tension or contradiction between diverse passages of the Bible, nor between the collections of Hebrew and Christian Scriptures that they called the Old and the New Testament. Leaders from different branches of the Protestant family tree debated endlessly over the finer matters of Christian doctrine and practice, but they did so by disputing their competing interpretations of their sacred text, not the authority of the text itself.

But this distinctly Protestant conviction that the truth of the gospel was singular and pure led inevitably to disputation and conflict. Across centuries English Protestants argued endlessly among themselves—and with Protestants on the European continent—over the question of who was interpreting

the Bible most accurately. Leaders from different sects of
English Protestantism embraced different ways of teaching and
practicing the faith, even as they professed their longings for
Christian unity. As they established various footholds in the
"New World" of North America, they confronted a kind of
cultural diversity that they were unable to imagine or comprehend. As the Bible began to pass through more and more hands,
its "gospel" was subject to an ever more varied interpretation.
The result, inevitably, was a perpetual propensity to what
scholars of religion call "schism"—branches, if you will, within
the Protestant family tree.

Understanding how this early English Protestant quest
for truth invited dissent, division, and separation can help
us understand the creative, innovative spirit that remains a
driving force in contemporary American life. It can also help
us understand why so many Americans today embrace their
own subjective experience as authoritative, rendering them
susceptible to propaganda and manipulation.

The Doctrine of Truth

As was the case on the European continent, the rise of Protestant
movements in England and the technological revolution of the
printing press were mutually reinforcing. As one dissenting
English clergyman summed things up toward the end of the
sixteenth century: "as Printing of Books ministered matter of
Reading, so Reading brought Learning, Learning showed Light;
by the brightness whereof blind Ignorance was Suppress'd,
Error Detected, and finally God's Glory with Truth of his Word
Advanced. And thus much for the worthy Commendation of
Printing."[1] But devout Protestants did not think of the Bible as
simply a container of knowledge. As suggested by the moniker
they gave to it—the "Word of God"—they considered it a revelation in and of itself, an oracle endowed with properties of
divine transcendence.

The first printing press was established in London in 1476, and at first printed Bibles were considered so valuable that they were chained to reading desks and pulpits in churches throughout England. Beginning in 1611 the translation commissioned and authorized by King James became widely available. As printing technologies improved across the ensuing generations, Bibles were reduced in size, eventually so much so that they could be held in the palm of a hand. Amazed at this technological miracle, devout English Protestants became transfixed by their Bibles, much as readers in the twenty-first century are transfixed by their handheld devices. Over time, the English became much more than mere readers of print. They came to use their Bibles, along with other cherished books like catechisms, prayer books, and psalters, not just for reading and reading aloud, and not just for just teaching and learning, but also for praying, singing, preaching, worshiping, writing, meditating, and so on. Somehow, devout English Protestants believed, the printed words on the pages of their sacred books connected them mysteriously to the life and death and resurrection of Jesus Christ.

Through an experiential encounter with the written Word, the Bible, individual Protestants understood that they could be put in touch directly with the living Word, as Jesus was described in the Gospel of John: "In the beginning was the Word, and the Word was with God, and the Word was God. . . . And the Word was made flesh, and dwelt among us, (and we beheld his glory, the glory as of the only begotten of the Father,) full of grace and truth" (John 1:1, 14, KJV). For all their many differences of doctrine and practice, early English Protestants agreed that the ultimate truth—the truth of the gospel—was obtained through the experience of this ultimate encounter.

In time some devout English Protestants concluded that the scriptural revelation required that individuals do more than merely accept, or even "understand," its message. To be saved from the powers of sin and death, individuals needed to apprehend or "receive" the gospel as it was presented to them, whether in printed or spoken form. Evidence of this salvation was found in the experience of "conversion," a momentous life change—a "dawning of the light"—and a subsequent profession of faith. This view found an early and powerful expression in Richard Baxter's *A Call to the Unconverted, to Turn and Live*, a combined treatise and prayer book that ran through dozens of editions from the time of its first publication in London in 1651. Baxter, an adherent of "nonseparatist" and yet "nonconforming" views, composed his *Call* "to be read in families where any are unconverted" and explained that an experience of conversion was a prerequisite to their eternal salvation: "All you that are yet Unconverted in this Assembly, take this as the undoubted Truth of God, you must e're long be Converted or Condemned, there is no other way but *turn or die*."[2] To Baxter it seemed obvious that this message could not be delivered by a preacher who had not experienced conversion himself. For this reason, Baxter counseled his readers, controversially, to go to their pastors "and acquaint them with your Spiritual Estate. . . . Or, if you have not a Faithful Pastor at home, make use of some other in so great a need."[3]

Encouraged to explore their own spiritual experience and to question their religious authorities, some devout Protestants arrived, inevitably, at the conclusion that the power of God's word could come directly—which is to say, unmediated—to individual believers. Raised in a dissenting Leicestershire family, George Fox launched the Religious Society of Friends, the movement that would come to be known as the Quakers, in 1647. Fox was convinced that only by opening themselves fully to the "inshinings" of the Light could the faithful inherit the essential promise of the gospel—"Ye shall know the Truth, and the Truth shall make you free" (John 8:32, KJV). And only then would they be able to live freely in obedience to the teachings of

Christ, as distilled in Christ's Sermon on the Mount. Quakers considered this conviction a logical extension of the quintessentially Puritan principle that the individual's relationship to God was paramount in the life of faith. It provoked rabid opposition, however, from more traditional Puritans, as well as from the broader community of dissent in England. Within a few years of its establishment, Fox's society began to explore colonization as an escape from this persecution, sending missionaries to both Europe and North America in the mid-1650s. The early Quaker experience in New England was not markedly different from what Fox's society had experienced in England, however, and, in short order, Quakers were being expelled—or martyred—by the Puritan authorities of the early New England colonies. From this experience Quakers on both sides of the Atlantic became rooted in their identity as a society forged in the crucible of suffering.[4]

As things turned out, Protestant assertions about the supreme authority of the Bible did not exempt them from the fundamental laws of human knowledge, what philosophers call "epistemology." As Hilary Gatti has summarized, the rejection of Roman Catholic tradition "required its substitution by some alternative source of truth, not only in the biblical word but in the human mind itself. The word of the Holy Scriptures could be claimed as the streaming fountain of all truth, but the question remained: how, and with what degree of certainty, could the Scriptures be interpreted and understood?"[5] As early English Protestants answered this question by looking inward, what they created was not a movement characterized by unity, but rather by extraordinary diversity. The experience of Pennsylvania, the first Quaker colony in the New World, was illustrative. From the time he brokered the colony's founding in 1681 to the time of his death in 1718, William Penn was convinced that his "holy experiment" in religious liberty should allow for the free shining of the pure light of the gospel, leading

naturally to social harmony among Quakers and non-Quakers
alike. In fact, Pennsylvania's commitment to freedom of religious expression produced a proliferation of divisions among
Pennsylvania Quakers—what the New York governor Thomas
Dongan in 1687 called "an abundance of Quakers . . . singing
Quakers, ranting Quakers, Sabbatarians, anti-Sabbatarians,
some Anabaptists, some Independants," and what Penn himself
decried as "scurvy quarrels that break out to the disgrace of the
Province."[6]

A new environment for public discourse in English-speaking
America was being created—eclectic to the point of chaotic,
individualistic to the point of idiosyncratic, contentious to the
point of acrimonious, prone to fundamental and irreconcil-
able differences not just of opinion, but of ways of seeing and
perceiving the world. Paradoxically, this same environment
made it possible for some savvy communicators to enjoy spectacular success in reaching wide audiences by reducing things
to the least common denominator.

A New Protestant Vernacular

Deeply convinced of the power of the printed word, the first
generations of Puritans who arrived in New England assumed
that access to the Bible and related print material was a cornerstone of their colonizing enterprise. In 1639 Reverend Jose
Smith contracted the locksmith Stephen Daye to operate his
Cambridge printing press, the first in North America. By the
turn of the eighteenth century, Boston was "home to 19 booksellers, who trafficked in both imported and locally printed
books, and seven publishing houses," according to David D.
Hall.[7] Most people in colonial New England encountered "a
limited number of books. Most had the use of, or owned, a Bible,
psalmbook, primer, and catechism. Almanacs were widely
available. Otherwise, the factors of cost and distribution were

barriers to extensive reading." The resultant mode of engaging with print material was characterized by intense scrutiny of a small group of texts that were treated as instruments of sacred communication.

Through the early decades of the eighteenth century, these core Protestant print materials reached a wider and wider audience, their distribution facilitated by the expansive geographic dispersal of the New England population and by the spread of print technology. Robust networks of print production spread from Boston to New York to Philadelphia in the first decades of the eighteenth century, and soon printing presses, or "houses" as they were commonly called, were established in every colony.[8] Eventually, Philadelphia overtook Boston and New York as the largest hub of print production, helping to establish its reputation as America's "First City."[9] Benjamin Franklin, whose career as a printer traced this entire arc, was the undisputed titan of this new transcontinental media landscape.

Born in Boston on January 17, 1706, Benjamin Franklin was apprenticed at the age of twelve to his older brother, James, a printer.[10] As was true elsewhere in colonial America, the publication of newspapers invited controversy in Massachusetts, and the practice of airing public controversy was deemed inherently oppositional by colonial authorities.[11] When James Franklin launched his own newspaper, *The New England Courant*, in 1721, it quickly earned a reputation as a vehicle for expression of protest and dissent.[12] In June 1722 the Massachusetts General Court jailed James Franklin for a "High Affront" to the colony's authorities, and in his absence, the sixteen-year-old Benjamin took editorial control of the *Courant*. Publishing spirited defenses of his brother under the pseudonym "Silence Dogood," Benjamin Franklin earned a reputation that would define his early career—in his own words, "as a young Genius that had a Turn for Libelling & Satyr."[13]

After a falling-out with his brother in 1723, Benjamin Franklin moved to Philadelphia at the age of seventeen. Following a sojourn in London, the ingenious and industrious Franklin returned to Philadelphia and established his own printing house, with contracts to publish official colonial business as its backbone. Soon, however, he embraced the publication of newspapers and almanacs, which would earn him both controversy and fame. In 1729, Franklin acquired *The Pennsylvania Gazette*, emblazoned its banner with a slogan promising the "freshest advices foreign and domestick," and filled its first pages with dispatches of news from both sides of the Atlantic.[14] The last pages, meanwhile, featured paid advertisements, dominated by announcements of runaway slaves, books for sale, and services rendered. Punctuating these standard offerings were occasional poems, often in the form of elegies and epitaphs, and announcements of deaths, the forerunners of the modern obituary. Typically, these were reserved for persons of some fame or repute, from queens and governors to poets and priests, comprising something of a celebrity-watch.[15]

Franklin's *Philadelphia Gazette* was viewed with continual suspicion by English authorities on both sides of the Atlantic.[16] Seeking to retain his contract with colonial authorities while simultaneously publishing criticism of them, Franklin continued to publish his own content using various pseudonyms, mixing it in with content produced by others, much of it unattributed. The result was a flood of information, the source and authenticity of which readers were unable to detect. Neither did Franklin limit himself to dispensing corroborated information. The convention of distinguishing between "fact" and "fiction" would emerge only slowly across the eighteenth century.

Benjamin Franklin marshalled defenses of the freedom of the press both philosophical and practical. He had long been enamored of a defense put forth by the publishers of the *London Journal*:

> Without Freedom of Thought, there can be no such Thing as Wisdom; and no such Thing as publick Liberty, without Freedom of Speech; which is the Right of every Man, as far as by it, he does not hurt or controul the Right of another: . . . Freedom of Speech is ever the Symptom, as well as the Effect of a good Government.

But he was also interested in turning a profit, as he was quick to admit. As he explained in his June 1731 "Apology for Printers," "Printers are educated in the Belief, that when Men differ in Opinion, both Sides ought equally to have the Advantage of being heard by the Publick; and that when Truth and Error have fair Play, the former is always an overmatch for the latter: Hence they chearfully serve all contending Writers that pay them well, without regarding on which side they are of the Question in Dispute."[17]

In 1732, Franklin launched his *Poor Richard's Almanack*, based on models he knew from his Boston upbringing.[18] As was true for other early American almanacs, the backbone of *Poor Richard's* was a series of monthly calendars, guiding the reader through the year with the days of the month listed in a first vertical column and successive columns containing days of the week, along with astrological information and their implications for the tides and weather. The calendars also included a listing of "days observ'd by the Church," including the days of saints and martyrs, and frequently a "Chronology of Things Remarkable," recounting a long string of events ordered by the number of "years past since the birth of Jesus Christ." The Chronology made clear that God was at work in human history, and preferentially so in Christian history. Even more specifically it made clear that God was providentially at work in the history of the English and their colonial experiment in North

America. Franklin's almanacs also featured the "man of signs," the image of the human anatomy connecting various parts of the body to the movement of celestial bodies, and a smorgasbord of prescriptions for physical ailments. Franklin advanced to a fine art the practice of filling what otherwise would have been white space atop, between, and amid the monthly calendars with poems, aphorisms, epitaphs, phrases drawn from Scripture, excerpts from hymns, and other miscellany.[19]

From the outset Franklin made clear to his readers that he was committed to publishing what he believed they wanted to hear. In the preface to the inaugural issue of his *Poor Richard's Almanack for the Year of Christ 1733*, Franklin, writing under the pseudonym Richard Saunders, forecast for his readers the death of his "good Friend and Fellow-Student, Mr. Titan Leeds." To predict someone's death was the holy grail of early astrology, which pretended to link the inner workings of the human body to the movements of the planets and stars. The following year, in the *Poor Richard's Almanack for 1734*, "poor Richard" professed ignorance as to whether his prediction from the previous year had been realized, but in his almanac for 1735, Franklin captivated his readers by confirming the death of the fictitious Leeds. In the edition for 1736, he reported to his readers that his earlier editions had "excited the Envy of some, and drawn upon me the Malice of others" because of "the great Reputation I gain'd by exactly predicting another Man's Death." In 1737 he defended his faulty predictions of the weather, asking his readers "only the favourable Allowance of *a day or two before* and *a day or two after* the precise Day against which the Weather is set." Lest his readers grow disgruntled with the uselessness of the forecasts, he invited them to take comfort in the fact that "his *Fi'pence* helps to light up the comfortable Fire, line the Pot, fill the Cup and make glad the Heart of a poor Man." Franklin was laughing all the way to the bank—the phenomenal growth of *Poor Richard's* made him a very rich man.[20]

The success of Franklin's *Poor Richard's* ushered in a new era in American publishing, their unique discourse helping to fashion what T. J. Tomlin has described as a "divinity for all persuasions." This brand of divinity provided a field of meaning bounded by a core set of essential Christian doctrines, such as the lasting influence of Christ's redemptive work on the cross and the assumed safe passage of the faithful to eternal life in heaven. As suggested by their mashing together of widely varied information from a diversity of sources, the publishers of almanacs did not consider "natural astrology" to conflict with the revelation of the Christian scriptures. Rather they believed the designs of providence made all these data points align, even if this alignment evaded the precise calculation of human beings.[21] The divinity for all persuasions of Americans remained articulated in what scholars recognize as a "Protestant vernacular tradition."[22]

From the outset of his career in Philadelphia, Benjamin Franklin sought to establish himself not just as a printer but also as an importer and seller of books, a practice that would become yet another successful branch of his publishing empire.[23] Franklin sold some new titles and also exploited the opportunity when demand for some "steady seller" made a local print run profitable. In 1729, in just his second year in business, Franklin determined that this was the case for Isaac Watts's *The Psalms of David, imitated in the language of the New Testament.*[24] As Franklin recognized, Watts was giving voice to a new style of Protestantism in North America that was proving spectacularly popular across gaps of culture, colony, and confession.

Like that of Franklin himself, Isaac Watts's genius lay in his ability to encapsulate the Protestant gospel without resorting to complicated language or controversial doctrine.[25] Watts set his lyrics to the most familiar "meters," making them easy for English speakers on both sides of the Atlantic to memorize and sing. Because they sounded so simple and natural, Watts's "hymns and spiritual songs" could be sung with great passion by large crowds in public spaces.[26] As William Dargan has so compellingly chronicled, Watts's unique blend of words and sounds also revolutionized the worship practices of the colonies' Black population, both slave and free.[27] Watts's compositions were perfectly suited to the tumultuous, freewheeling atmosphere of America's growing cities and inspired a host of imitators.[28]

Because of their familiarity, popularity, and ease of singing, Isaac Watts's lyrics were also popular among traveling, or itinerant, evangelists, who grew more and more connected across the middle decades of the eighteenth century. Conjuring William Baxter's *Call to the Unconverted*, these preachers emphasized the spiritual necessity of a "new birth" or "awakening."[29] Working independently of any strict denominational affiliation or theological program, these preachers launched an array of movements that many historians lump together as a "Great Awakening." Taking to the emerging public squares of the colonies with animated speeches, orations, sermons, and pronouncements, they helped create what Richard Cullen Rath has described as a new American "soundscape," in part by "claiming their own voices as God's thunder."[30] Looming as a giant over this network was the itinerant Anglican evangelist, George Whitefield, and standing ready to assist him was Benjamin Franklin.[31]

George Whitefield opened what would become his legendary second visit to America in Philadelphia, and Benjamin Franklin was among the many who remembered it as a momentous occasion. On November 8, 1739, Whitefield delivered a sermon to a crowd that Franklin estimated as six thousand, a number approximating half of Philadelphia's settled population. Above all, what Franklin remembered was *hearing* something altogether startling and unique. Whitefield's delivery, Franklin observed, was "so improved by frequent repetition, that every accent, every emphasis, every modulation of voice, was so perfectly well-tuned, and perfectly placed, that without being interested in the subject, one could not help being pleased with the discourse."[32] As the home of a thriving publishing industry, and with a reliable port connecting both cargo and passengers to every major destination on both sides of the Atlantic, Philadelphia became the North American hub of Whitefield's evangelistic operation, and he retained his close collaboration with Franklin and his associates until his death in 1770.

Benjamin Franklin is rightly portrayed by his biographers as a quintessential skeptic and iconoclast and a leading light in the rise of modern science, his religious views squarely within the fold of an ascendant Deism that characterized God as a supremely rational being. Across decades he helped to establish Philadelphia as the central node of an intercolonial network of science, arts, and letters.[33] In 1743—inspired in part to contest the expanding role played by the Anglican Church's Society for the Propagation of Christian Knowledge—Franklin formed the Society for Useful Knowledge, calling for "virtuosi or ingenious men residing in the several colonies" to share the fruits of the intellectual and technological labors. After the 1751 publication of his *Experiments and Observations on Electricity*, Franklin was awarded honorary degrees by both Yale and Harvard and the Copley Medal, the Royal Society of London's highest honor. Franklin had become a *bona fide* and uniquely multidimensional celebrity on both sides of the Atlantic, a kind of Elon Musk for the eighteenth century.

But through it all, Franklin flooded the American public square with the ideals of early English Protestantism as these had been adapted to their distinctive circumstances in North America. With Franklin's assistance, Isaac Watts, George Whitefield, and their many imitators fashioned a new American way of thinking and speaking and singing that spread throughout the colonies across the middle decades of the eighteenth century. This American vernacular was grounded in ideals of masculine virtue, rooted in a distinctively Protestant brand of moralism, and facilitated the spread among leading colonists of a shared sense of divinely sanctioned purpose. This new way of thinking encouraged the English in North America to think of themselves as "American," but it would also lead them to think about themselves as "white," informed by residual Puritan and Quaker self-understandings as a suffering and victimized people.[34] More and more, English colonists began to use the designations "white" and "American" interchangeably, contrasting themselves not just with their growing slave populations, and not just with the Native peoples of the mid-Atlantic region, but also with immigrants from Germany, Scotland, Ireland, and other parts of Europe.

In 1751, the same year he published *Experiments and Observations on Electricity*, Franklin also published *Observations Concerning the Increase of Humankind*. In these observations, Franklin scanned the globe, commenting in ways that baffle our modern perceptions. Observing that "the Number of purely white People in the World is proportionably very small," he elaborated:

> All Africa is black or tawny. Asia chiefly tawny. America (exclusive of the new Comers) wholly so. And in Europe, the Spaniards, Italians, French, Russians and Swedes, are generally of what we call a swarthy Complexion; as are the Germans also, the Saxons only excepted, who with the English, make the principal Body of White People on the Face of the Earth. I could wish their Numbers were increased.

Steeped in the cosmopolitan culture of Philadelphia, where both slave-owning and emerging abolitionist sentiment coexisted peacefully, Franklin's objections to the African slave trade were not moral, but aesthetic:

> And while we are, as I may call it, Scouring our Planet, by clearing America of Woods, and so making this Side of our Globe reflect a brighter Light to the Eyes of Inhabitants in Mars or Venus, why should we in the Sight of Superior Beings, darken its People? why increase the Sons of Africa, by Planting them in America, where we have so fair an Opportunity, by excluding all Blacks and Tawneys, of increasing the lovely White and Red? But perhaps I am partial to the Complexion of my Country, for such Kind of Partiality is natural to Mankind.[35]

This self-understanding—an aspiring and expansive colonial enterprise, imbued with a sense of divine destiny, cast in racialized terms—would soon be embraced by English speakers across colonial British North America. Through ever-thickening networks of intercolonial print communication, the colonists discovered a new collective sense of self-understanding, one that was fashioned over and against their erstwhile neighbors. In a least common denominator, but still very Protestant, vernacular, the English in North America were creating an ethnonationalist identity.

Join or Die

As tensions continued to mount through the first half of the eighteenth century, leaders from across the English colonies in North America began to fashion a coordinated response to counter the growing threat posed by French and Indian collaboration. In 1752, Benjamin Franklin published his woodcut image of a segmented snake, each segment labeled as one of England's nine northern colonies. On the front page of his *Pennsylvania Gazette*, he captioned the image, "JOIN, OR DIE." In May 1754, just as formal hostilities were breaking out between England and France, delegates from seven British colonies in North America gathered in Albany, New York, for

what would come to be known as the "Albany Conference."
While the conference did not produce a formal declaration of
union, it helped strengthen a network of colonial publishers,
who began to exchange news in the form of excerpts and
reprints in local newspapers. These included not just battle-
field accounts and other reports from the ever-shifting front
lines but also calls-to-arms, commonly cast in the generic
Protestant vernacular that Benjamin Franklin and others were
making so popular. The image of Franklin's snake proved a hit
in this network, circulating widely in the ensuing war, often
re-captioned, "UNITE OR DIE."[36]

Sermons lauding the war effort also received wide distribution through this same network. In *A Short Address to Persons of
All Denominations*, George Whitefield encouraged the faithful
to put aside any reservations about the war, first citing precedents from "Antient History" and then "those heroic Worthies"
cited in Scripture, "who by Faith subdued Kingdoms, and put to
Flight the Armies of Aliens." Whitefield grounded his appeal in
the martial inheritance of English Protestantism: "the British
Arms were never more formidable than when our Soldiers
went forth in the Strength of the Lord, and with a Bible in one
Hand, and a Sword in the other." Placing his own generation
in this long tradition, Whitefield argued that "if God himself
is pleased to stile himself a Man of War, surely a just and righteous Cause (such as the British War at present is) we may as
lawfully draw our Swords, in order to defend ourselves against
our common and public Enemy, as a civil Magistrate may sit on
a Bench, and condemn a public Robber to Death." Describing
himself as "fully convinced of the Justice of the British Cause,"
Whitefield declared the outbreak of war a "happy misfortune,"
arguing:

> For, surely, it is far more preferable to die, tho' by a Popish
> Sword, and be carried from the Din and Noise of War by
> Angels into Abraham's Bosom, than to be suffered to survive,

only to drag on a wearisome Life, and to be a mournful Spectator, and daily Bewailer, of one's Country's Ruin.

Whitefield begged his audiences to read "the shocking Accounts of the horrid Butcheries, and cruel Murders committed on the Bodies of many of our Fellow-Subjects in *America*, by the Hands of savage Indians, instigated thereto by more than savage Popish Priests." There was no reason to think, he explained, "that Rome, glutted, as it were, with Protestant Blood, will now rest satisfied." Originally preached and published in London in early 1756, by the end of the year Whitefield's sermon ran through six editions in North America in the hands of Benjamin Franklin and other printers in Philadelphia, New York, and Boston.

Benjamin Franklin also championed the literary career of John Dickinson, a man whom later generations of historians would dub "the penman of the Revolution." Dickinson was born on November 8, 1732, in Talbot County, Maryland, into one of Pennsylvania's earliest Quaker families. Raised for much of his youth in Kent, Delaware, Dickinson trained as a lawyer in London and in 1757 returned to establish a successful law practice in Philadelphia. Dickinson was as cultured and cosmopolitan as Franklin, if not nearly so famous. His transatlantic legal training, his literary pedigree, and his rise to prominence in Pennsylvania politics gave him a unique vantage on the process by which a "continental" identity was emerging in North America. As this same process drove a wedge between the colonists and their king in the aftermath of the French and Indian War, Dickinson gave early voice to growing "American" resentment.[37]

John Dickinson's *Letters from a Farmer in Pennsylvania* were first published anonymously by Franklin's associate David Hall in Philadelphia in 1768. The *Letters from a Farmer*, as they came to be known, laid out a rationale for a united, intercolonial opposition to the Townshend Acts, a series of revenue-enhancing measures the English Parliament had approved as an intended compromise after Americans had so loudly protested the Stamp Act. Dickinson understood the essential concerns shared across the colonies and articulated these concerns in the terms that represented increasingly common discourse among colonial elites:

> Let these truths be indelibly impressed on our minds—that we cannot be HAPPY, without being FREE—that we cannot be free, without being secure in our property—that we cannot be secure in our property, if, without our consent, others may, as by right, take it away—that taxes imposed on us by parliament, do thus take it away—

For those less philosophically inclined, Dickinson summarized the case more bluntly: "Those who are taxed without their own consent, expressed by themselves or their representatives, are slaves. We are taxed without our consent, expressed by ourselves or our representatives. We are therefore—SLAVES."[38] The *Letters from a Farmer* were reprinted multiple times in Philadelphia, Boston, and New York and circulated widely throughout the colonies.

John Dickinson also wrote—and Franklin's Philadelphia associate, David Hall, also printed—what later historians would call America's "first hit song."[39] At first published anonymously like his *Letters from a Farmer*, Dickinson's *A New Song* was also distributed widely, beginning in 1768. By year's end, it had come to be known as the "Liberty Song" and had grown so popular it could be casually mentioned from Connecticut to Virginia as "so justly admired thro' all North-America."[40]

> Come join hand in hand, brave Americans all,
> And rouse your bold hearts at fair Liberty's call;
> No tyrannous acts, shall suppress your just claim,
> Or stain with dishonor America's name.

CHORUS: In freedom we're born, and in freedom we'll live;
Our purses are ready, Steady, Friends, steady,
Not as slaves, but as freemen, our money we'll give.

Our worthy forefathers—let's give them a cheer –
To climates unknown did courageously steer;
Thro' oceans to deserts, for freedom they came,
And, dying, bequeath'd us their freedom and fame.
CHORUS

. . . .

Then join hand in hand brave Americans all,
By uniting we stand, by dividing we fall
In so righteous a cause let us hope to succeed,
For Heaven approves of each generous deed.
CHORUS

All ages shall speak with amaze and applause,
Of the courage we'll show in support of our laws;
To die we can bear, - but to serve we disdain,
For shame is to freedom more dreadful than pain.
CHORUS

It is no coincidence that Dickinson's *Liberty Song* spread so readily through the colonies—its structure of repeating eleven-syllable lines was among the most familiar meters, and Dickinson wrote the lyrics to be sung to the tune *Hearts of Oak*, an explicit counter to the anthem of the British Royal Navy. Christopher Boyd Brown has documented that "Singing the Gospel" was part and parcel of the popular religious upheaval that culminated in the Protestant Reformation, and Laura Mason has shown that French peasants in the 1790s were "Singing the French Revolution."[41] So, too, American colonists in the 1760s and 1770s went singing their way to independence from the British Crown—and the beat of their revolutionary song was distinctly Protestant.

Neither is it coincidence that the signature line of the *Liberty Song*—commonly shorthanded as "united we stand or divided we fall"—would become one of the revolution's most famous slogans, for it echoed the sentiment popularized by Benjamin Franklin's famous snake. After the French and Indian War concluded in 1763, Benjamin Franklin's image of a segmented snake was picked up by champions of inter-colonial opposition to Britain's postwar policies of trade and taxation. And beginning in 1774, colonial newspapers from Isaiah Thomas's *The Massachusetts Spy* to William Bradford's *The Pennsylvania Journal* emblazoned Paul Revere's version of the snake on their mastheads in support of the revolutionary cause. For this reason, people rightly recognize it as a powerful symbol of the American Revolution. But Franklin created his snake long before he even considered the possibility that the colonies might separate from England. The snake that Franklin portrayed was threatened by the hated Catholic French and their Native American allies. The original American snake was white and Protestant, and the people John Dickinson called "brave Americans" knew it.

Innovation and Propaganda

The men who launched the English print enterprise in North America believed that truths large and small were contained in their sacred scriptures. At first the spread and advances of print technology facilitated the intercolonial distribution of a core set of material that had proven popular in Puritan New England. Across the middle decades of the eighteenth century, though, the freewheeling environment of Philadelphia attracted printers and other "creatives" in unprecedented numbers, helping to establish it as the center of cultural production in North America. An explosion of creativity was facilitated by the (originally Quaker) notion that truth was in the eye—or "inner light"—of the beholder. This same notion blurred the boundaries between denomination, culture, and class and turned the city into a hotbed of controversy and contestation. Philadelphia became a case study in what Zac Gershberg and Sean Illing call the "the paradox of democracy: a free and open communication environment that, because of its openness, invites exploitation and subversion from within."[42] Alongside Boston, Philadelphia became a center of revolutionary ferment.

Benjamin Franklin mastered this early American media environment through his publication of *The Pennsylvania Gazette* and *Poor Richard's Almanack*, among other publications, and through his prolific distribution of the works of Isaac Watts, George Whitefield, and others who helped shape a new American "soundscape." Dozens of printers followed—or attempted to follow—the template Franklin set. Through the middle decades of the eighteenth century, the technology of the printing press continued to advance, allowing publishers to print an ever larger number of pages. Improvements in roads and bridges facilitated travel and correspondence between colonial populations, allowing printers to share their work more expeditiously with one another. Information of all kinds ricocheted around the colonies with ever-increasing velocity, to the marvel of successive generations.[43] Individuals, especially in major urban hubs, experienced the flood of information as overwhelming, even more so because they had no real means of assessing the veracity of information promulgated from so many sources. Many traditionalists, including colonial authorities, considered the print enterprise inherently threatening to public order and stability, as they had from the beginning of the colonial experience.[44] Most everyone agreed that the media environment was unruly, acrimonious and encouraged Americans to barricade themselves into warring "factions." Today Americans call them "bubbles."

Benjamin Franklin is rightly recognized as a chief author of an emerging American national identity, but most commonly for his work with the other men who crafted the Declaration of Independence and the US Constitution. Celebrated as a religious iconoclast, a technological and scientific revolutionary, and a free-thinker extraordinaire, he is perhaps the favorite among all the founders among American liberals today. And understandably so.

But the print network that Franklin helped to catalyze in the generations leading up to it may have been his most impactful contribution to the American Revolution. And through this network Franklin promoted a least-common-denominator vernacular that rooted English speakers from across the colonies in their shared Protestant identity. In this new vernacular the descriptors "white" and "American" came to be considered virtually synonymous and were widely understood to refer to people of English and Protestant descent. In a famous 1943 article, "The Revolutionary Press—A Social Interpretation," Sidney Kobre summarized that the medium of print "helped develop 'a consciousness of kind,' an emotional, intellectual and economic sympathy for distant colonies."[45] This consciousness of kind also included the embrace of an ethnonationalist identity.

The American commitment to freedom of expression is rooted in the early Protestant belief that the free press was an instrument of propagating the truth. This commitment inspires innovation and creativity, but it also renders American consumers of media susceptible to propaganda. As was true in the buildup to the American Revolution, so too today ingenious content creators reach across a fractious media environment by generating simple, easy-to-apprehend messages in written, spoken, and visual forms. Successful "influencers" today are commonly innovative, inventive, lyrical, and unafraid to offend. Many are passionate and principled and dedicated to a deeper understanding of what is truth. Many others are arrogant, self-righteous, moralistic, and willfully propagandistic. The "genius" that Benjamin Franklin displayed as he launched his career as a publisher/propagandist is harder to come by than what he described as his "Turn for Libelling & Satyr."

As did our revolutionary forebears, Americans today have trouble discerning what is and is not true. I can wish that my discernment was always true. But I recognize that I, like most Americans, live more and more in a "mediated" environment. Over the years I have uploaded, liked, and spread my share of opinion on social media, and of course the designers of the algorithms at Facebook and Twitter were happy to feed me more of what I like. I remain a fan of the online comment boards at the *New York Times* and the *Washington Post* and delight as the wittiest take downs filter to the top as "most liked." I know that on other platforms I would not like the most-liked comments at all.

All this is inevitable given the free speech we cherish as Americans. Innovation is the sweet fruit of the American search for truth, but we have not learned how to curb our desire for propaganda, the bitter fruit that springs forth from this same root.

Susceptibility to ethnonationalist propaganda is a deep root of white Christian nationalism. Staffers on the House Select Committee charged with examining the role played by social media in facilitating the January 6, 2021, attack on the US Capitol concluded that "alt-tech, fringe, and mainstream platforms were exploited in tandem by right-wing activists to bring American democracy to the brink of ruin. These platforms enabled the mobilization of extremists on smaller sites and whipped up conservative grievance on larger, more mainstream ones." Had he been asked to comment, I imagine the mature Benjamin Franklin weighing in with what he wrote to a friend in 1767: "New Men, and perhaps new Measures are often expected and apprehended, whence arise continual Cabals, Factions and Intrigues among the Outs and Ins, that keep every thing in Confusion. And when Affairs will mend, is very uncertain."[46]

CHAPTER 5

Liberty
Independence and Conspiratorial Thinking

English Protestants conceived of human history as an epic and all-encompassing struggle between good and evil, between life and death, between light and darkness. As Jesus himself had declared, "I am the light of the world: he that followeth me shall not walk in darkness, but shall have the light of life" (John 8:12, KJV). In this way of thinking, human life is a contest, a protest, a battle, and a stark, zero-sum game, with the light of individual (Protestant) liberty under perpetual threat from the forces of tyrannical darkness. In the worldview of early English Protestantism, this threat was ubiquitous, with the shape-shifting Satan able to exercise tyrannical influence both supernaturally and through a host of human actors, sometimes unwitting dupes and sometimes knowing accomplices. The truly faithful were expected to carry forth the light of the gospel, even knowing that their enemies would be unceasing in their efforts to extinguish it.

The idea that the English colonists thought they were bringing the light of the gospel into lands filled with darkness is familiar to most Americans today, owing largely to the enduring popularity of an image conjured by John Winthrop in his 1630 sermon, *A Modell of Christian Charity*. In this sermon, Winthrop quoted the prophet Isaiah: "and then shall thy light brake forth as the morning and thy health shall grow speedily, thy righteousness shall go before God, and the glory of the Lord shalt embrace thee" (Isaiah 58:6, 8). Characterizing the colonial venture as of "mutual consent through a special overruling providence," he declared to his companions aboard the ship *Arbella*, "we shall be as a City upon a Hill." Winthrop's powerful image has been embraced and repurposed down through the generations, from successive generations of Protestant preachers to American presidents as diverse as Franklin Delano Roosevelt and Ronald Reagan, who declared America "a shining City on a Hill."[1]

Shaped by this spiritual inheritance, many English colonists in North America considered the struggle to protect their liberty as being played out at every level, from the inner spiritual lives of individuals to the collective lives of their congregations, communities, and colonies right up to and including the English church and Crown. In this way of thinking, the more the power exercised by corrupt civil or religious authorities, the lesser the "liberty" enjoyed by individuals and, necessarily, the greater the threat of "tyranny." Many leaders of the American Revolution cast the struggle for American Independence in precisely these terms. Two and a half centuries later, this essential framing dominates the social media feeds of millions of Americans.

Understanding how early English Protestants thought of liberty and tyranny can help us make sense of Americans' deep devotion to individual freedoms. It can also help explain the propensity to conspiratorial thinking by which Americans today are perpetually tempted.

The Doctrine of Liberty

As a part of their generations-long rebellion against the Roman Catholic Church, early English Protestants strung themselves along a spectrum of resistance to their own national church, the Church of England. Some simply refused to "conform" to the dictates of Anglican authorities, while others actively "dissented" from them. Some sought to "reform" the church, while others, more devout, aspired to "purify" it. The most radical English Protestants saw the Anglican bishops—like the English royalty who consecrated them—as hopelessly entangled with Roman Catholic institutions, authorities, and ideologies. These radicals concluded that Christians wanting to live pure lives needed to "separate" themselves not just from Rome but also from London. Some English radicals sought to establish "separatist" and "puritan" communities while remaining in England. Others sought refuge in distant lands, from the Netherlands to North America.

Wherever they sat on this spectrum of dissent, early English Protestants understood the freedom to propagate the gospel of Jesus Christ as contained in their sacred scriptures to be the essence of "Protestant liberty." This liberty consisted of several foundational freedoms—the freedom of Protestant printers to print the Bible and related material (the freedom of the press), the freedom of Protestant clergymen to preach and teach as they saw fit (the freedom of the pulpit), and the freedom of Protestant individuals to both practice and profess their faith (the freedoms of conscience and speech). All Protestants agreed that these liberties required zealous protection, for they understood the spread of the gospel to be the very dynamic by which God was at work in human history.

As early English Protestants thought about it, the exercise of these liberties required continual vigilance and contestation because authorities both civil and ecclesiastic routinely exercised undue authority—or "tyranny"—over their subjects. English Protestants felt this way of thinking was confirmed by their recent history. As summed up by John Foxe, the famed English martyrologist, Protestant liberty was threatened by "tyranny of three kinds, viz., that which enslaves the person, that which seizes the property, and that which prescribes and dictates to the mind." This third kind, which Foxe called "ecclesiastical tyranny," was the "worst kind of tyranny, as it includes the other two sorts." The Catholic popes were the very epitome of this total tyranny, which was in turn the true desire of the "Romish clergy" who "not only do torture the bodies and seize the effects of those they persecute, but take the lives, torment the minds, and, if possible, would tyrannize over the souls of the unhappy victims."[2]

In this rendering, the English Civil Wars of the mid-seventeenth century were just part of a much longer and protracted resistance to Catholic assaults on true Christian liberty. This resistance culminated in what came to be called "the Glorious Revolution," which inaugurated the reign of the Protestants William and Mary in 1688 and enshrined the English Bill of Rights the following year. The Bill of Rights opened with an accusation leveled at the Catholic monarch, King James II: "By the assistance of divers evil counsellors, judges and ministers employed by him," it asserted, James "did endeavour to subvert and extirpate the Protestant religion and the laws and liberties of this kingdom." This depiction of James as a tyrant was followed by a litany of complaints. The Bill of Rights then resolved that the Protestants "William and Mary, prince and princess of Orange, be and be declared king and queen of England, France and Ireland and the dominions thereunto belonging."

Influenced by the rising tide of the Enlightenment, more and more English philosophers began to derive their arguments in support of religious liberty and other freedoms from what they assessed to be the "laws of nature" and "natural rights." As John Locke articulated in his *Two Treatises on Government*, published in 1689—the same year as the English Bill of Rights—good government should be founded only to protect and preserve these rights and the right of "every Man" to "Property in his own Person" most proximately: "The great and chief end therefore, of Mens uniting into Commonwealths, and putting themselves under Government, is the Preservation of their Property." Among the "property" that freedom-loving Englishmen needed to "preserve" from government interference were their tongues. As explained by the authors of the *London Journal*: "This sacred Privilege is so essential to free Governments, that the Security of Property, and the Freedom of Speech always go together; and in those wretched Countries where a Man cannot call his Tongue his own, he can scarce call any Thing else his own. Whoever would overthrow the Liberty of a Nation, must begin by subduing the Freeness of Speech."[3]

English Protestants on both sides of the Atlantic took arguments like these not as challenges to Protestant orthodoxy, but rather as buttresses to it. After all, the two great sources of knowledge—the "laws of nature" and the "revelation of Scripture"—were not perceived by faithful Protestants as countervailing forces. On the contrary, they were seen as pushing in the same direction. For the devout Protestants, the "natural liberty" proclaimed by the rising tide of Enlightenment philosophy was identical to the Protestant liberty for which their forefathers had fought and died. And this liberty was inherently jeopardized by the formation of governments, no matter their form. As Locke summarized, "where-ever the Power that is put in any hands for the Government of the People, and the Preservation of their Properties, is applied to other ends, and made use of to impoverish, harass, or subdue them to the Arbitrary and Irregular Commands of those that have it: There it presently becomes Tyranny, whether those that thus use it are one or many." Independent-minded leaders in the English colonies of North America would come to think of their Revolution in this dual spotlight.

A Diabolical Conspiracy

The first generations of English to settle in what they called New England were among the most radical of early English Protestants. As they saw it, their yearning for liberty required them to "separate" from the undue influence of the English Crown and church. As the famed Puritan clergyman Cotton Mather would later reminisce, they aimed "to seek a place for the exercise of the Protestant Religion, according to the light of their consciences in the deserts of America."

Mather's romantic reminiscence notwithstanding, the Puritans' search for religious freedom proved more complicated than they ever imagined. The first generations of New England colonists attached preposterous expectations for Indian evangelization to early publications like the Eliot Bible, a printed Bible translated into the Narragansett tongue by the Puritan John Eliot. Translation of other catechetical material soon followed, including excerpts from Richard Baxter's *A Call to the Unconverted*, which were translated into Algonquin and printed in Massachusetts colony as early as 1664. But the dissemination of the Christian gospel did not naturally and peaceably convert the residents of the North American "wilderness," and the English in New England were soon overwhelmed by their new circumstances. Leaders in colonial New England concluded they had not removed themselves from the power of Satan, the ultimate enemy of Christian freedom and an expert in the arts of manipulation. In time the English in North America came to think of themselves as an embattled people, perpetually vulnerable to threats from within and without.[4]

The threat from without was exemplified by the threat of Indian raid-making and captive-taking. Common Native practices, honed across generations of intertribal warfare, included surprising enemy settlements and killing any who might compromise the arduous journey that captivity would invariably demand. Native raid-makers typically killed adult male captives, who were expected to resist; any women who could not be incorporated into the new tribe by force, by accommodation, or by a combination of the two; and all those thought to lack mobility and endurance, such as the elderly and small children. Older children, meanwhile, made for especially attractive captives—they could travel quickly with adults, readily establish new relationships with peers, and were often naturally adept at acquiring new languages and customs. Culturally mandated rites of incorporation, such as running the gauntlet and ritual washing, were effective in identifying young captives amenable (or susceptible) to these strategies of cultural accommodation. As they came of age, moreover, young captives were likely to establish attachments of affection to members of the opposite sex that made for a powerful incentive to acculturate.

The threat of captivity at the hands of the Indians seemed even more menacing to the English because their principal colonial competitors, the French, were more adept at forging alliances with the continent's Native peoples. Most French explorers established relations with Indian tribes in North America through trade, a basis far less threatening than the English quest for the proprietary acquisition of land. But this simple understanding was lost on the English colonists, who considered French success in this regard evidence of their treachery. The English saw being taken captive by Indians as synonymous with being trafficked into the domains of demonic popery. The English heralded Indians like the Patuxet Tisquantum (nicknamed "Squanto" by his English kidnappers in New England) and the Powhatan Motoaka (more popularly known as "Pocahontas" in Virginia) for seeming to hold out proof—or at least the possibility—that the Protestant enterprise in North America might someday transform the New World's Native peoples into good Englishmen. But while the English thought it right to take captives as prisoners of war— or even slaves—for the most part they lacked the acquired skill of incorporating them into English culture. By the turn of the eighteenth century, the English in New England were of a common mind: the wilderness of North America was the fertile ground of a diabolical conspiracy.

Surrounded by the French and the Indians, the English in North America came to think of themselves as an embattled people, perpetually vulnerable to physical, ideological, and spiritual captivity. They felt this vulnerability most viscerally as they considered their wayward young. The idea that Indians were not just taking young people captive but were actively absorbing them as full members of their tribes horrified the English colonists. And the thought that these tribes were in league with the hated French elevated their concern even further. In 1699, when he was taken captive by Maliseet Indians at the age of ten from his hometown of Pemaquid, Maine, the last words John Gyles recalled hearing from his mother were these: "If it is God's will, I had rather follow to your grave, or to never see more in this world than you should be sold to a Jesuit. For a Jesuit will ruin you body and soul."[5]

An Aggravated Tyranny

Across the middle decades of the eighteenth century, as networks of intercolonial communication and correspondence continued to thicken, English Protestants in colonial America came to think of themselves as the rightful heirs to the Glorious Revolution of 1688 and the English Bill of Rights, the champions of true liberty. In the aftermath of the French and Indian War, leaders from across the colonies discovered shared resentments of royally appointed magistrates, whom they saw as exercising increasing and unaccountable authority over colonial governments and institutions. In 1765 the physician Benjamin Church heralded the theme that would become the rallying cry of more and more Bostonians:

> Fair LIBERTY our soul's most darling prize,
> A bleeding victim flits before our eyes:
> Was it for this our great forefathers rode
> O'er a vast ocean to this bleak abode!
> When *liberty* was into contest brought,

And loss of life was but a second thought;
By pious violence rejected thence,
To try the utmost stretch of providence;
The DEEP, unconscious of the furrowing keel,
Essay'd the tempest to rebuke their zeal;
The tawny natives and inclement sky
Put on their terrors, and command to fly;
They mock at danger; what can those appall
TO whom fair LIBERTY is all in all.[6]

Just as it had been the place where the seed of Puritanism was planted in American soil, and just as it had been the birthplace of the American print enterprise, Boston would become the cradle of the American Revolution.

Organizing under the banner of the "Sons of Liberty," a small network of radicals from within Boston's elite led protests against the Stamp Act of 1765, the British Parliament's first effort to tax the colonists, and the Townshend Acts of 1767, through which Charles Townshend, then chancellor of the Exchequer, attempted to impose duties on the colonies' trade. Using the "Liberty Tree" as a rallying point, they aligned themselves with disaffected merchants, building on long-standing resentments of working-class artisans, laborers, and apprentices. In 1773 the Tea Act galvanized Bostonians' opposition—most famously in what would come to be known as the Boston Tea Party—as did the "Coercive Acts" (called the "Intolerable Acts" by most American colonists) and the "Quartering Act," requiring Bostonians to foot the bill for housing British troops.[7] Throughout, the Sons of Liberty provided a steady stream of content to local Boston publishers, galvanizing an increasingly coordinated resistance to the new postwar regime.[8]

No one embodied this network of resistance more completely than Samuel Adams. While a student at Harvard, Adams and a group of fellow students launched a newspaper called the *Independent Advertiser*, which exalted New England's Puritan heritage while expressing open mistrust of Massachusetts's

colonial authorities.[9] Channeling ancient Protestant preoc-
cupations with individual liberty and governmental power,
Adams earned a master's degree by writing on the question of
"whether it be lawful to resist the Supreme Magistrate, if the
Commonwealth cannot be otherwise preserved." Calling into
question the doctrine known as the "divine right of kings,"
Adams answered this question in the affirmative, and he took
this spirit of resistance with him into public life.

In 1764, in anticipation that postwar taxes would soon
be imposed by the British Parliament, Adams drafted the
"Instructions of the Town of Boston to Its Representatives in
the General Court." Adams laid out his views in radical terms
that conjured John Locke:

> if our Trade may be taxed why not our Lands? Why not the
> Produce of our Lands? Why not the Produce of our Lands &
> every thing we possess or make use of? This we apprehend
> annihilates our Charter Right to govern & tax ourselves. . . .
> If Taxes are laid upon us in any shape without having a legal
> Representation where they are laid, are we not reduced from
> the Character of free Subjects to the miserable State of tribu-
> tary Slaves?[10]

But Samuel Adams also conjured John Foxe, the founding
father of English Protestant martyrology. Adams asserted that
New England had been established by people who were "persecuted in England at a Time when the Nation was intoxicated
with Bigotry & the Ideas of Ecclesiastical Tyranny." As articulated by Adams, this inheritance inspired in Bostonians a deep
reverence:

> When we recollect the ardent love of Religion and Liberty,
> which inspired the Breasts of those Worthys; which induced
> them at the Time when Tyranny had laid its oppressive Hand
> on Church and State in their Native Country, to forsake their
> fair Possessions and seek a Retreat in the distant Part of the

Earth—When we reflect upon their early care to lay a solled Foundation for Learning, even in a Wilderness, as the surest means of preserving and cherishing the Principles of Liberty and Virtue, and transmitting them to us their Posterity, our Mind is filled with deep Veneration and we bless and revere their Memory.[11]

In time an entire cadre of American revolutionaries would come to share Adams's view that taxation without representation both "annihilated" the political rights of Americans as English subjects and struck at the very foundation of their spiritual inheritance as heirs to the Glorious Revolution and the English Civil War.

In a series of December 1768 articles for the *Boston Gazette*, Adams argued that the quartering of British troops in Boston confirmed John Locke's saying, "Where Law ends, TYRANNY begins, if the Law be transgress'd to another's harm."[12] The spirits of Bostonians, however, were "as yet unsubdued by tyranny" and were "unaw'd by the menaces of arbitrary power" and would never "submit to be govern'd by military force."[13] Believing that "the law . . . rightly used, is the curb and the terror of the haughtiest tyrant," Adams was, at this stage, still convinced that New England's magistrates would "execute the good and wholesome laws of the land with resolution and an intrepid firmness." Still, he counseled his fellow Americans:

That constitution which admits of a power without a check, admits of tyranny: And that people, who are not always on their guard, to make use of the remedy of the constitution, when there is one, to restrain all kinds of power, and especially the military, from growing exorbitant, must blame themselves for the mischief that may befall them in consequence of their inattention.[14]

That same year, Adams and others began to publish a "Journal of Occurrences," a newsletter from Boston that was excerpted in nearly every newspaper in colonial America. The journal portrayed the suffering of Bostonians at the hands of British troops. This "martyrdom" of Boston was not just a predicament, but rather "an American problem."[15] In October 1769, his optimism waning, Adams once again conjured England's sacred memory in an article for *The Gazette*:

> Let any one imagine the distress of this people—a free city, I mean once free and still entitled to its freedom, reduc'd to the worst of tyranny—an aggravated tyranny! Was not an army of placemen and pensioners sufficient, who would eat us up as they eat bread, but an array of soldiers must be stationed in our very bowels—Where is the bill of rights, magna charta and the blood of our venerable forefathers! In this dilemma to what a dreadful alternative were we reduc'd! To resist this tyranny, or, submit to chains.[16]

The American Revolution was set to launch.

King George, The Tyrant

In the years leading up to the American Revolution, colonial elites forged a newfound sense of shared purpose. This purpose was rooted in a spirit of opposition that was endemic to early English Protestantism. Across generations on both sides of the English Civil War, devout Protestants had characterized "tyranny" as a multidimensional threat. The spirit of tyranny could seize control of the hearts and minds of individuals, or it could take hold of local civic and ecclesiastical authorities. It could infect political parties and high-ranking government officials. English Protestants considered this spirit to be the work of Satan, and they believed its aim was to extinguish Protestant liberty. As Bernard Bailyn observed in his landmark 1967 *The Ideological Origins of the American Revolution*, "the fear of a comprehensive conspiracy against liberty throughout the English-speaking world . . . lay at the heart of the Revolutionary movement."[17]

In its most dangerous expression, this spirit of tyranny could possess people in high places, including popes and kings. Generations of English-speaking Protestants in North America had been trained to think of the pope as a beastly tyrant who must be opposed at all costs. But English kings had never been immune from the wrath of English Protestants inclined to cast all their struggles in stark, all-or-nothing terms. It had happened before in the years of the English Civil Wars, and reminders of these battles still coursed through the popular culture. The leap from thinking of popes and kings and queens as tyrants to rejecting monarchy altogether was not such a long leap, it turns out. As Thomas Paine summed things up in his phenomenally popular pamphlet, *Common Sense*, "the Almighty hath here entered his protest against monarchical government.... For monarchy in every instance is the Popery of government."[18]

The revolutionary movement launched through the early 1770s reached a climax on June 7, 1776, when the Continental Congress appointed a committee of five to prepare a Declaration of Independence: Thomas Jefferson of Virginia, Benjamin Franklin of Pennsylvania, Roger Sherman of Connecticut, Robert Livingston of New York, and John Adams of Massachusetts. By this time John Adams was well established as a leader of the Congress, but he was convinced that Jefferson should make the first draft of a declaration. Jefferson was a Virginian and—as Adams would recall later in his autobiography—had been elected to Congress in larger part for having authored *A Summary View of the Rights of British America*, a 1774 essay "which had given him the Character of a fine Writer." Adams also considered Jefferson's relative lack of exposure an advantage. Just thirty-three at the time, Jefferson had not represented Virginia at the first Continental Congress, convened in 1774. He had participated actively, but unremarkably, in the opening sessions of the second Continental Congress in late 1775, and he had arrived late at its spring sessions in 1776. He had fought few battles in Congress, and a draft drawn by his hand was likely to be met with less preconceived opposition. Thomas Jefferson did not disappoint John Adams's expectations, and his draft, as amended and improved by his fellow committee members, was approved by the Congress on July 2, 1776.

Because its opening phrases are so graceful, it can be easy to overlook the way the preamble of the Declaration of Independence connects to its larger argument. The way Jefferson rendered it, the "unalienable Rights" of the American colonists were gravely threatened by a single, tyrannical figure, England's King George III.

In his 1774 Summary View of the Rights of British North America, Jefferson had opined that "bodies of men, as well as individuals, are susceptible of the spirit of tyranny," but he had linked this threat to the British Parliament and to the injustice that "160,000 electors in the island of Great Britain should give law to four millions in the states of America"—"parliamentary tyranny," he called it. But in the Declaration of Independence, Jefferson escalated and dramatized the confrontation, concentrating the threat of tyranny in a single person: "The history of the present King of Great Britain is a history of repeated injuries and usurpations, all having in direct object the establishment of an absolute Tyranny over these States." Replicating the essential structure of the English Bill of Rights, Jefferson followed with a lengthy list of these "injuries and usurpations," written in the eighteenth-century equivalent of bullet-point form. This listing was book ended by another, even more direct accusation leveled at King George III: "A Prince whose character is thus marked by every act which may define a Tyrant, is unfit to be the ruler of a free people."

Not all members of the drafting committee were comfortable with this strident approach. As late as 1774, leading revolutionaries were professing ardent loyalty to King George III and attempting to keep the focus of Americans' ire on the British Parliament.[19] John Adams wrote later, "there were other expressions which I would not have inserted if I had drawn it up, particularly that which called the king tyrant. I thought this too personal; for I never believed George to be a tyrant in disposition and in nature. I always believed him to be deceived by his courtiers on both sides of the Atlantic, and in his official capacity only, cruel. I thought the expression too passionate, and too much like scolding, for so grave a solemn document." Most historians today would agree with John Adams's assessment that George III was merely the front man of British policy in North America.[20] But Thomas Jefferson understood that the fundamental purpose of the Declaration was persuasion, not analysis. So he embraced the strident propaganda of Samuel Adams, rather than the lawyerly argumentation of John Adams. This strategy was roundly approved by the delegates to the Continental Congress.

The key argument of the Declaration of Independence—that King George III had become a "tyrant"—was steeped in Protestant pathos and suspicion. By casting the American predicament as a stark and simple confrontation between individual liberties and a tyrannical ruler who had seized control of the apparatuses of power, Jefferson tapped a stream of oppositional Protestantism that reached back centuries. This way of thinking required that resistance to a monarch (or "prince") be predicated on his possessing the character of a tyrant.

Benjamin Franklin tapped this same stream of discourse the next month in his draft of a "Great Seal" for the new nation, the one with an image showing Pharaoh being vanquished by the parting of the Red Sea.[21] Franklin's proposal included the motto "Rebellion to Tyrants is Obedience to God." The proposal was not adopted by the Congress, but Thomas Jefferson loved the motto so much that he later used it on his own personal seal.

Historians of early America continue to expand their understanding of the diverse sources of colonial discontent and how these sources galvanized around common themes to create a revolutionary movement. The discontents of many were rooted in the ancient Protestant suspicion that concentrations of authority, whether civil or ecclesial, were invitations to the abuse of power. As Mark Noll has summarized, the revolutionaries saw such abuses of power as constituting inherent threats to the exercise of individual liberty, and they considered the exercise of individual liberty an essential precondition to "the potential for virtue in a society."[22] For many who led and fought in it, the American Revolution was a fight to protect not abstract Enlightenment ideals, but the very same virtue and liberty heralded by their Protestant ancestors.

Independence and Conspiratorial Thinking

The challenge of establishing purified Christian communities in North America proved more daunting than leading New England colonists ever imagined. Over time they came to think of themselves as confronting not just the inherent weakness of the human condition but also the influence of dark and malevolent forces, from both within and without. They were victims of a diabolical conspiracy. Across the span of centuries, this sense of pervasive threat and embattlement has remained a constant in the American psyche, with white Christian Americans from every generation conceiving of themselves as vulnerable to persecution by powerful forces both seen and unseen. These sensations of threat, persecution, and mistrust are enduring fruits of the American founding. White Americans often experience these sensations most acutely when they see their young exposed to forces beyond their comprehension or control.

Many Americans today perceive themselves to live as far removed from the metropolitan centers of power as the American revolutionaries did from London. Many consider the impersonal bureaucracies of the federal government, directed and managed by imperious liberal elites, not as instruments of social reform and progress, but, fundamentally, as threats to individual liberties. Many cannot conceive of American public life except as a perpetual struggle to protect these liberties, especially the religious liberty that Protestants hold most dear—the liberty to print and preach and proclaim what they want, where they want. This is what many Americans mean today when they say they believe the United States was founded as "a Christian nation." They believe the United States was destined to stand as the vanguard of individual liberty, construed in distinctly Protestant terms.

These resentments, suspicions, and aspirations can be traced to the very deepest roots of the American founding, and Americans who still harbor them today can find ample encouragement in the writings of the nation's founders. Indeed, these sentiments saturate the writings of people like Samuel Adams and John Dickinson and the speeches of men like Joseph Warren and Patrick Henry. The presumption that behind British colonial policy lay King George's thirst for absolute tyranny forms the backbone of our nation's most cherished document, the Declaration of Independence. US presidents will forever be cast as insatiable tyrants by their opponents, for Americans shaped by the inheritance of English Protestantism will forever suspect that unchecked power leads inevitably to its concentration in the institutions of government and its absolute concentration in the hands of powerful individuals holding high office.

This mistrust is shared by Americans ranging from radical libertarians on the Right to devotees of the American Civil Liberties Union on the Left. It shapes popular movements as diverse as the Proud Boys and Abolish ICE. It fuels vaccine conspiracies across the ideological spectrum. It shapes the way most Americans think about politics and is put on regular display by ordinary citizens from all walks of life in city council meetings and school board hearings throughout the nation. So independent-minded as to be ready to fight for what they believe to be right, so suspicious of people in positions of authority as to perceive every wrong as the fruit of conspiracy—these attitudes are as American as apple pie. Conspiratorial thinking is a bitter fruit of the American founding, and it will continue to flourish because, by their very nature, conspiracy theories are difficult to disprove.

It is little wonder that Jacob Chansley—a.k.a. Jake Angeli, a.k.a. the "QAnon Shaman"—became a kind of icon for the January 6, 2021, insurrection. Chansley was at the head of the group who, after entering the Capitol, celebrated their surprising success at gaining access to the chamber of the US Senate. Images of Chansley offered a peculiar kind of comfort: they allowed us to think of the mob that stormed the US Capitol, "Maybe they are just plain crazy."

But when Chansley removed his bearskin cap, grabbed his bullhorn, and shouted, "Let's pray!" he delivered an entirely coherent invocation. Chansley's prayer employed some language that is standard in conservative American Christian circles— he twice addressed God as "Heavenly Father," for instance. And on three occasions he evoked the New Age theme of God's "white light" of love. Fundamentally, though, Chansley's invocation was rooted in a distinctly American brand of early English Protestantism. Chansley encapsulated this tradition neatly on January 6, opening his prayer by thanking God for "this opportunity to stand up for our God-given inalienable rights." He concluded by declaring:

Thank you for allowing the United States of America to be reborn.
Thank you for allowing us to get rid of the communists, the globalists,

and the traitors in our government. We love you and we
    thank you.
In Christ's holy name we pray.

Dozens of Chansley's co-conspirators responded with emphatic
shouts of "Amen!" Millions of more white American Protestants
would have shouted the same had they been there.

Few Americans may share Jacob Chansley's precise mix of
conservative evangelicalism, New Age philosophy, and QAnon
conspiracy theories. But millions share with him the fundamentally dualistic and oppositional and ethnonationalist way
of thinking that provided the architecture for his impromptu
invocation. In the view of these millions of Americans, the presidential election of 2020 resulted in a cataclysmic outcome—
powerful elites with tyrannical aspirations have once again
seized control of the instruments of government. That efforts
to overturn the 2020 election results did not come to frui-
tion merely means that God has not finished with America
yet. More radical action is required to save America, to bring
America back from the edge of death.

Shortly after the January 6 insurrection, an old friend
with whom I rarely talk politics asked about my book on
martyrdom and the making of the American Revolution. I
gave him a nutshell description of early English Protestantism
and described how it lends itself naturally to conspiratorial
thinking. I explained how this way of thinking leads many
Americans to suspect that the people in power are always
turning into tyrants. My friend chuckled and said, "Kind of
like some people think about Trump, huh?" I had not thought
of it in those terms, but my friend's comment gave me pause.

I considered how preoccupied I had become with the
singular figure of Donald Trump during his tenure in office. To
be clear, I consider Trump to have been the worst president in
my lifetime. I believe he broke countless laws in attempting to

overthrow the constitutional order of the United States, and I hope that someday he will be held accountable for doing so. As I write today, I consider his recently declared candidacy for the 2024 presidential election a tragedy for our nation. But I marvel at how I have allowed so much of my attention to became concentrated on this single man.

I was disappointed when the House Select Committee charged with investigating the events of January 6, 2021, fell prey to this same temptation. By choosing to focus their attention so uniquely on Trump's role in the insurrection, they failed to place the events of that day in larger contexts. As Jill Lepore has summarized: "In the January 6th Report, Donald Trump acted alone and came out of nowhere. He has no past. Neither does the nation. The rest of the country doesn't even exist." The January 6 Committee erred in reducing the root causes of the January 6 insurrection to a "Big Lie," in Lepore's estimation:

> "The Big Lie" is not a big lie. It is an elaborate fiction, an artful story, with heroes and villains, exotic locales, and a sinister plot. The election was stolen by a cabal of Democrats, social-ists, immigrants, criminals, Black people, and spies . . . it is the latest chapter in a fictive counter-history of the United States which has been told by the far right for decades upon decades upon wretched decades.

In fact, it is a fictive counter-history that white Americans have been telling themselves for centuries.[23]

Now I recognize that in my fixation on Donald Trump I fell prey to a very American style of conspiratorial thinking. By imagining the evils of white racism and xenophobia to have their origins in a single powerful man, I comfort myself with the thought that removing the man from power will resolve the matter. But Donald Trump is much more a symptom of American disease than he is the cause of it. Trump is not best understood as an outlier, as a single individual who egregiously violated institutional norms. He is much better understood as the latest in a long lineage of salesmen hawking white Christian nationalism. Trump picked up the mantle of Joe McCarthy, George Wallace, and Pat Buchanan, to be sure. But white nationalists like these were merely riffing off a brand of white grievance politics that has always been a powerful force in American politics. Whatever fate befalls Donald Trump—whether he ends up back in the White House, is sentenced to federal prison, or simply returns to his prior profession of media manipulation—his brand of politics is not going away. This brand is too American to hope or expect that it will disappear from America's public life.

CHAPTER 6

Virtue
Patriotism and Nationalism

Early English Protestants understood the death and resurrection of Jesus Christ to be the crux of human history. In submitting to death on the cross, Jesus offered himself in self-sacrifice for the forgiveness of all human sins. "Herein is love, not that we loved God, but that he loved us, and sent his Son to be the propitiation for our sins" (1 John 4:10, KJV). As a reward for his faithfulness on the cross, God raised Jesus from the dead, and those who proved faithful to him would share in his resurrection. As the Apostle Paul wrote to the early Christian community in Rome: "For if, when we were enemies, we were reconciled to God by the death of his Son, much more, being reconciled, we shall be saved by his life" (Romans 5:10, KJV). This was the Bible's core message, the "gospel," or good news, as early English Protestants understood it: as foretold by the Hebrew prophets, Jesus was the "Christ," the anointed one of God (the word "Christ" in Greek being a translation of the Hebrew word, "Messiah"). In his crucifixion God offered every human being a release from the stranglehold of sin, and in his resurrection the promise of deliverance from the greatest tyrant of all, the tyrant death.

The way early English Protestants thought about it, the miracle of print had made the truth of the Gospel, as found in the pages of the Bible, transparent and available to all. The life of faith, then, was a struggle to conform one's life and death to that of Jesus—to "shew forth the Lord's death till he come" (1 Corinthians 11:26, KJV).[1] As a part of this struggle, the truly faithful should stand ready to witness to the truth, even at the pain of death. Exemplary of this faith were the Protestant martyrs, who followed in the footsteps of Jesus, the one who "humbled himself, and became obedient unto death, even the death of the cross" (Philippians 2:8, KJV).

Understanding the deep roots of English Protestant martyrdom, and how this tradition was adapted and appropriated to the cause of the American Revolution, can help us understand the enduring power of patriotism in American life. It can also help us understand more fully the powerful temptation of white Christian nationalism.

The Protestant Doctrine of Virtue

The way early English Protestants conceived of it, the whole of human history had culminated in a battle between Protestant truth and Roman Catholic ritual, pageantry, and superstition. As were their European counterparts, English Protestants were repulsed by the suggestion that participating in the Roman Church's sacraments was necessary to salvation. They found especially abhorrent the Catholic doctrine professing there to be a "real presence" of Christ's body and blood in the sacrament. Like so much else of Catholic teaching, they considered this "hocus pocus" (a pejorative derived from the declaration in the Latin Mass, *hoc est corpus*, meaning "this is the body"). Instead, most English Protestants considered what they called "the Lord's Supper" to be simply "a memorial" of the death of Christ.

Even as they bickered among themselves continually over the finer matters of doctrine and practice, most English Protestants simply took for granted that the Roman popes were the agents of Satan on earth, forever conspiring to extinguish the truth of the gospel. And even when their national church, the Church of England, and the English monarchy were headed by nominal Protestants, they remained susceptible to Roman manipulation. For this reason, true Protestants must remain vigilant, they thought, and stand ever ready to resist established authorities, both civil and ecclesiastic. Early English Protestants took for granted that sometimes this resistance would require the ultimate sacrifice from the truly faithful.

Although most Americans today associate the word "martyrdom" with other religious traditions, the concept was central to the self-understanding of early English Protestants. As they waged what they understood to be an all-or-nothing war against the Catholic popes, they traced the lineage of their own martyrs back across the ages to the martyrs of the early church.[2] This early Christian tradition was shaped profoundly by Greek understandings of bearing testimony (the word *martyrios* in Greek means "witness") and by the Roman understanding that the born male (*mas* in Latin) could become a true man (*vir*) through displays of masculine virtue (*virtus*). In this ancient way of thinking, the most striking display of virtue was made by those who witnessed the truth even when confronted by death.[3] Jesus's death on the cross represented the touchstone of this tradition. Jesus was "the faithful witness and the first begotten of the dead" (Revelation 1:5, KJV). Those who followed his example of willing self-sacrifice became witnesses, or martyrs, to the truth.

The early English Protestant embrace of this tradition included not just acts of martyrdom themselves but also the curation of narrative and commemorative traditions around them—that is, martyrology—and the practices of spiritual formation by which the young were immersed in these traditions as part of their coming of age. Every act of martyrdom is both a death and a story about a death, and every story about a death holds the potential of inspiring the young to new acts of martyrdom.[4] Early English Protestants were expert in these arts of celebrating acts of martyrdom and preparing their young to battle valiantly to the death, assured that the truly faithful would be "crowned" with heavenly glory.[5] While true martyrs were usually men, and were hailed by English Protestants as paragons of masculine virtue, even women could exemplify these ideals.[6]

Entirely representative of this absolutist early Protestant worldview was John Foxe's *Actes and Monuments of These Latter and Perilous Days, touching matters of the Church,* first published in 1563. Foxe began chronicling the lives and deaths of England's Protestant martyrs during the brief, five-year rule of England's Catholic Queen Mary I (1553–58), a reign of terror for which her opponents nicknamed her "Bloody Mary."[7] The way Foxe saw it, the "true Church of Christ" was an inherently oppositional body that resisted Catholic assaults on true Christian liberty. Although this "true Church" was routinely "oppressed by tyranny" and suffered long periods of persecution, "some remnant always remained," personified by the martyrs who "stood in open defense of truth against the disordered Church of Rome."[8] Foxe lauded John Wycliffe, for instance, an early English translator of Scripture whose "observant mind penetrated into the constitution and policy of Rome." Before his martyrdom, Wycliffe "inveighed in his lectures, against the pope—his usurpation—his infallibility—his pride—his avarice—and his tyranny":

> He was the first who termed the pope Antichrist. From the pope, he would turn to the pomp, the luxury and trappings of the bishops, and compared them with the simplicity of primitive bishops. Their superstitions and deceptions were topics that he urged with energy of mind and logical precision.[9]

Another of Foxe's most famous profiles was of William Tyndale, who translated the Bible directly from the original languages, Hebrew and Greek, making possible the printing of the first complete English Bible in 1535. Burned at the stake the next year by King Henry VIII, Tyndale's dying words, as portrayed by Foxe, were, "Lord—open the King of England's eyes," conjuring countless stories from Scripture.[10]

In what came to be known simply as the "Book of Martyrs," Foxe crafted his tales, many accompanied by woodcut illustrations, as substitutes for the Roman Catholic legends of the medieval saints, piling them one on top of the next, casting them always against a scriptural backdrop. In one of his most famous accounts, John Foxe portrayed the Protestant English Bishop Hugh Latimer exhorting his colleague Nicholas Ridley as the two men were burned on a pyre at the instruction of Queen "Bloody Mary" in 1555. Turning to his younger colleague, Latimer proclaimed: "Be of good comfort Master Ridley, and play the man: we shall this day light such a candle by God's grace in England, as (I trust) shall never be put out."[11]

Foxe's phrasing would find its way into the King James Bible, first published in 1611, where it appeared in multiple places, including in the second book of Samuel, where the warrior Joab challenged his fellow Israelites as they prepared for battle against the Syrians: "Be of good courage, and let us play the men for our people, and for the cities of our God" (2 Samuel 10:12, KJV).[12] This phrase, to "play the man," captured succinctly the ancient association of martyrdom and masculinity, communicating clearly that the preparedness to die was a signal marker of masculine virtue and spiritual maturity. Good English Protestant boys were raised to understand that they would need to prove their masculine virtue by performing acts of bravery, even at the risk of their lives. In today's vernacular, they were taught that, if they lived long enough, sooner or later they would have to "man up" and perhaps even "take it like a man."

All parties to the conflicts of the English Civil Wars of the mid-seventeenth century tried to stake their claims as the rightful inheritors of the church's martyrological inheritance. Following the death of King Charles I in 1649, his followers heralded him as "King Charles the Martyr" and celebrated him as such on January 30 each year. This legacy was kept powerfully alive by Jeremy Taylor. Even before he published his twin volumes, *Holy Living* and *Holy Dying*, Taylor's devotion to the ideals of martyrdom were well established. In 1649, while serving as chaplain to Charles I, Taylor published a biography of Jesus, *The great exemplar of sanctity and holy life according to the Christian institution described in the history of the life and death of the ever blessed Jesus Christ the savior of the world.* Throughout his life, Taylor remained focused on Jesus's death as the heart of the gospel, resulting in the posthumous publication of *Antiquitates christianae, or, The history of the life and death of the holy Jesus as also the lives acts and martyrdoms of his Apostles: in two parts.*[13] For Taylor, fearlessness in the face of death, inspired by the promised joys of heaven, was the truest sign of fully realized Christian faith. This faith was exemplified by the saints and martyrs: "God could not chuse but be pleased with the delicious accents of martyrs, when in their tortures they cried out nothing, but Holy Jesus, and, Blessed be God."[14]

The first waves of English Protestants to colonize North America brought with them across the Atlantic their ancestors' understanding of human history as an epic and all-encompassing struggle between good and evil, between life and death. They also inherited their ancestors' oppositional spirit and their devotion to the ideal type of martyr, and they bequeathed this spirit and devotion to their descendants.

Leading Anglicans, Separatists, Baptists, and Quakers in early New England routinely pointed to their favorite martyrs as evidence that their own tradition represented the authentic Christian faith. In the eighteenth century, others would join this crowded field of contestation, including German Lutherans and Moravians, Anglican dissenters and Methodist itinerants, Anabaptists of many different kinds, French Huguenots, and Scots-Irish Presbyterians. Elites enthralled with ideas born from the Enlightenment found tales of martyrdom in their cherished "classics" of Greek and Roman antiquity. Everyone in colonial North America could link their spiritual heritage to a long lineage of martyrs, and everyone could see themselves in what they called "the martyr's mirror."[15]

Primed for Martyrdom

Protestants from across the theological spectrum in colonial America embraced the early Protestant martyrs as exemplars of true Christian faith, even though few would face circumstances requiring them to become martyrs themselves. Extreme encounters with death—such as those experienced in battle, shipwreck, plague, pregnancy, and execution—were commonly perceived to conjure the death of Christ himself and portrayed as having repercussions not just on a personal and familial, but on a social and even cosmic, scale. But even deaths that might otherwise be characterized as "ordinary" were commonly attributed importance in these other dimensions, depending on the conduct of the dying and the dispositions of those who witnessed the death. The scriptural accounts of Jesus's crucifixion served as the *de facto* template for accounts of deaths of every imaginable kind.[16]

As he did with so many things, Isaac Watts gave voice to this part of the English Protestant tradition, including the longing of even ordinary Protestants to be caught up in the larger sweep of the divine struggle against the powerful forces of death. Watts set "A Prospect of the Resurrection" to the common meter of alternating eight- and six-syllable lines (8.6.8.6):

> How long shall death, the tyrant reign,
> And triumph o'er the just,
> While the dear blood of martyrs slain
> Lies mingled with the dust?
> . . .
> O may my humble spirit stand
> Amongst them clothed in white!
> The meanest place at His right hand
> Is infinite delight.
> . . .
> How will our joy and wonder rise,
> When our returning king
> Shall bear us homeward through the skies
> On love's triumphant wing!
> . . .
> Great Babylon, that rules the Earth
> Drunk with the Martyrs' blood
> Her crimes shall speedily awake
> The Fury of our God.[17]

To English Protestants in colonial America, the lyrics of Watts stood out as a powerful, and scripturally grounded, endorsement of their cause. Everyone understood that the "Great Babylon" to which Watts referred was the Roman Catholic Church, and the blood she was drunk on was Protestant blood.

The grooming of young men for acts of martyrdom was an essential part of this American tradition.[18] Print materials designed specifically for the instruction of the young in colonial America routinely celebrated martyrdom as an ideal type of death. As did their forebears, English Protestants in early America raised their children to understand that the self-sacrificing deaths of the martyrs were the highest, and paradigmatic, expressions of true Christian faith and the surest way to earn the reward of eternal salvation. They taught them to understand that their immediate forefathers and ancient heroes risked martyrdom by standing up for their faith, defending their honor and virtue, and risking their lives at sea, in battle, or in confrontations with tyrannical authorities. They trained them to be ready for that time, sure to come, when they, too, might need to risk their lives as a rite of passage to manhood.

No book beyond the Bible was more widely distributed in British North America than the *New England Primer*, first published in Boston sometime before 1686.[19] Derived from Benjamin Harris's *Protestant Tutor*, an "early reader" popular among English Protestants, *The New England Primer* featured a pictured alphabet, each letter accompanied by an image and a simple rhyme, beginning with "A—In Adam's fall, We sinned all." With this alphabet, parents taught their young children to read while simultaneously preparing themselves for confrontations with the power of death, which they understood could come calling at any moment:

> G—As runs the Glass, Man's life doth pass. . . .
> R—Rachel doth mourn, For her first born. . . .
> T—Time cuts down all, Both great and small. . . .
> X—Xerxes the great did die, And so must you and I.
> Y—Youth's forward slips, Death soonest nips.

The *Primer* also included standard catechetical material like the Lord's Prayer and the Ten Commandments and the prayer that many early English Protestants taught their children to pray each night before going to bed: "Now I lay me down to sleep / I pray the Lord my soul to keep / And should I die before I wake / I pray the Lord my soul to take." Apart from the Lord's Prayer (the "Our Father . . . "), this prayer would remain the most familiar in the English language for centuries, and many English-speaking Protestants can conjure parts of it from memory even today. Generations of American children were put to bed to the reminder that they might not live to see the morning.

The capstone to the *New England Primer* was an adapted excerpt from Foxe's *Book of Martyrs*, often labeled simply "Martyrology." The featured martyr was "Mr. John Rogers, Minister of the Gospel in *London . . .* the first Martyr in Queen *Mary's* Reign, and was burnt at *Smithfield, February 12th, 1552.*" That John Rogers was given a place of such prominence is no surprise. As the first to be martyred under the reign of the notorious Bloody Mary, Rogers had also been given special treatment in Foxe's *Book of Martyrs*, and the illustrations of his martyrdom were among the most elaborate in each edition of Foxe's martyrology. In the *New England Primer*, the tale called "Martyrology" was typically accompanied by a dramatic woodcut illustration of Rogers tied to a stake, his body being consumed by the flames.[20] What many referred to simply as "the Primer" remained the most widely available children's book in British North America, straight down through the period of the American Revolution.[21] The first story that generations of colonial children read on their own was the story of a devout Protestant delivering a virtuoso performance of martyrdom for his faith.

This spiritual formation shaped the coming-of-age experience for young colonial men, who prepared to go to war as a foundational rite of passage. Catechized in the varied expressions of English Protestantism, most understood this rite of passage to be a matter of faith. As it had to their forefathers, the prospect of war presented to these young men an opportunity to demonstrate their masculine virtue and honor. Most considered war to be an intrinsically Protestant struggle against the French, whom the English took to be agents of Satan himself, and against the Indians, whom they viewed as at once inherently savage and at the same time capable of extraordinary bravery.

Many tribes in North America had expectations for how those taken captive in battle should behave that were analogous to English expectations of martyrs. "Braves," as the English came to call them, fulfilled the highest expectations of masculinity, refusing to show weakness and at times even seeming to relish execution as if they were putting one over on their enemy.[22] Young English colonists were raised to match their fervor, to prepare themselves spiritually for the possibility that honor and virtue might require them, in a moment of crisis, to "play the man."

Generations of young English colonists were given the opportunity to realize this ideal as they waged a near-perpetual war with their erstwhile neighbors. That the "savage" Indians and "diabolical" French were so frequently allied with one another inspired leading English colonists to forge intercolonial alliances of their own. During the mid-eighteenth-century French and Indian War, a shared ethos of masculine virtue, exemplified by the ideal of martyrdom, helped colonists to join forces across divides of colony, culture, class, confession, and creed. Exemplary deaths such as that of James Wolfe, the British major general who died as troops under his command secured a crucial victory in the 1759 battle of the Plains of Abraham, outside Quebec City, helped cement the colonists' commitment.[23]

As the mid-century war spread across North America, leading English colonists took up the fight in fine Protestant fashion—as a holy war. Thinking of themselves as fighting on the front lines of a cosmological battle, Protestant clergy in British North America preached hundreds of "muster sermons" to mobilize local militia, "battle cry" sermons to send troops into battle, and "memorial sermons" to commemorate the fallen. The Presbyterian Samuel Davies, who was introduced in chapter 3, was an exemplary practitioner of this tradition.

Beginning in 1755, Davies preached rabidly in support of the war, and his printed sermons spread through the burgeoning network of colonial print production. Davies had spent nearly a decade building dissenting congregations in Virginia, and the war presented him the rare opportunity to demonstrate his virtue and patriotism to the colony's Anglican elite. In August 1755, preaching to a volunteer company of the Hanover County militia, Davies delivered *Religion and Patriotism the constituents of a good soldier*, a sermon based on 2 Samuel 10:12, the verse with roots buried deep in centuries of English martyrology: "Be of good Courage, and let us play the Men, for our People, and for the Cities of our God: And the Lord do that which seemeth him good." Grossly misrepresenting the early history of Virginia as "An Hundred Years of Peace and Liberty," Davies declared that "now the Scene is changed.... Our Territories are invaded by the Power and Perfidy of *France*; our Frontiers ravaged by merciless Savages, and our Fellow-Subjects there murdered with all the horrid Arts of Indian and Popish Torture." Lest his listeners and readers remain uncertain about the nature of the threat confronting them, he went on to characterize Virginians as innocent victims and their Indian enemies as demons:

> The bloody Barbarians have exercised on some of the most unnatural and leisurely Tortures; and other they have butchered in their Beds, or in some unguarded Hour. Can human Nature bear the Horror of the Sight! See yonder! The hair Scalps, clotted with Gore! The mangled Lims! The ript-up Women! The Heart and Bowels, still palpitating with life, smoking the Ground! See the Savages swilling their Blood, and imbibing a more outragious Fury with the inhuman Draught! Sure these are not Men; they are not Beasts of Prey; they are something worse; they must be *infernal Furies* in human shape.

Enjoining the Hanover militiamen to join the cause not for provincial concerns, but as an expression of their faith, Davies asked rhetorically: "Shall Virginia incur the guilt, and the everlasting shame, of tamely exchanging her liberty, British liberty, her religion, and her all, for arbitrary Gallic power, and for Popish slavery, tyranny and massacre?"[24]

In 1756, Davies preached *Virginia's Danger and Remedy*, assessing the threat in dramatic terms: "Indian savages and French Papists, infamous all the World over for Treachery and Tyranny, should rule Protestants and Britons with a Rod of Iron." He asked Virginians, "Can you bear the Thought that Slavery could clank her Chain in this Land of Liberty?" That same year he justified his fervor in another sermon, *The Meditorial Kingdom and the Glories of Jesus Christ*, elaborating on the nature of the enemy confronting the British:

> This is the great mystical Babylon which was represented to St. John as drunken with the blood of the saints, and with the martyrs of Jesus, Rev. xvii.6. In her was found the blood of the prophets, and of the saints, and of all that were slain upon the earth, Ch. Xviii.24. And these scenes of blood are still perpetrated in France, that plague of Europe, that has of late stretched her murderous arm across the wide ocean to disturb us in these regions of peace. There the Protestants are still plundered, chained to the gallies, broken alive upon the torturing wheel, denied the poor favor of abandoning their country and their all, and flying naked to beg their bread of other nations.

And on May 8, 1758, in *The Curse of Cowardice*, a sermon addressed to a company of Virginia militiamen in the French and Indian War, Davies declared: "God grant you may return in Safety and Honour, and that we may yet welcome you Home, crowned with Laurels of Victory! Or if any of you should lose your Lives in so good a Cause, may you enjoy a glorious and blessed Immortality in the Region of everlasting Peace and Tranquility!"[25] Davies's tenure in Virginia earned him such a reputation that in 1759 he succeeded Jonathan Edwards as president of the College of New Jersey, later to become Princeton University.

Patriotism, This Most Noble Sentiment

The English Protestant tradition celebrating martyrdom as the paradigmatic expression of masculine virtue played a key role in the spiritual formation of America's revolutionary generation.[26] As English colonists became more and more connected to each other through the growing network of print publication and distribution, they discovered they shared the belief that the fullest expression of Christian virtue was to lay down one's life for a sacred cause. And in the years leading up to what would become the War of Independence, more and more arrived at the conclusion that the American cause was such a cause, a cause worth dying for.

On February 20, 1770, an angry crowd of Boston youth gathered outside the shop of Theophilus Lillie, a Boston merchant accused of violating the Nonimportation Agreement, a boycott protesting British taxes of imports to the American colonies. When Ebenezer Richardson, a British customs official, came to Lillie's defense, the mob turned their ire on him and followed him home. There Richardson fired on the crowd, injuring one and mortally wounding another, Christopher Seider, aged eleven. The next week, the publishers Benjamin Edes and John Gill announced a funeral procession in the February 26 edition of their *Boston Gazette and Country Journal*, the city's oldest newspaper:

> he will be buried from his Father's House in Frogg Lane, opposite Liberty-Tree, on Monday next, when all the Friends of Liberty may have an Opportunity of paying their last

Respects to the Remains of this little Hero and first Martyr to
the noble Cause.

On the very same day that this account appeared in the *Gazette*,
March 5, 1770, British troops opened fire on the protesting
crowd, killing three young men onsite and mortally wounding
two more.

In the years following the incident that would come to be
known as "the Boston Massacre," the Sons of Liberty worked
diligently to keep the memory of their young martyrs alive. At
annual commemorations on the anniversary, March 5, notable
Bostonians delivered public orations, which were then circulated in print by the Boston Town Council. John Hancock, the
son of Samuel Hancock, one of Boston's wealthiest merchants,
delivered the address in 1774.

Like those who had gone before him, Hancock identified the
quartering of British troops in the city as the proximate cause
of what they called "the horrid massacre." But this was not
the only theme that Hancock shared with his fellow orators.
Like the others, he also conjured the memory of the colony's
ancestors, celebrated them for their demonstrations of fearlessness in the face of death, and challenged their listeners to carry
this legacy forward. Portraying the unfortunate victims of
the bloody massacre as passive victims, Hancock saw another
possibility "which I behold in countenances of so many in
this great Assembly." This alternative was "Patriotism . . . this
noble affection which impels us to sacrifice everything dear,
even life itself, to our country." Conjuring the familiar motif of
"playing the man," and asserting the ultimacy of divine judgment, Hancock declared, "I have the most animating confidence that the present noble struggle for liberty will terminate
gloriously for America. And let us play the man for our God,
and for the cities of our God." By the end of the following year,
Hancock's speech had been published not just in Boston but

also in New Jersey, Rhode Island, and Pennsylvania.[27] On March 5, 1775, John Warren conjured the legacy of English Protestant martyrdom in his second public oration marking "the horrid massacre," but this time with a special sense of urgency. Insisting that "Where justice is the standard, Heaven is the warrior's shield," Warren declared:

> Our country is in danger, but not to be despaired of. Our ene-
> mies are numerous and powerful, yet we have many friends;
> determine to be free, and Heaven and Earth will aid the
> Resolution. . . . Your fathers look from their celestial seats with
> smiling approbation on their sons, who boldly stand forth in
> the cause of virtue.[28]

Just weeks later, on April 19, Massachusetts militia resisted efforts by British troops to seize caches of arms at Lexington and Concord, marking the outbreak of formal hostilities. On June 17, some 140 soldiers in the Massachusetts Provincial Army—and perhaps twice as many British troops—were killed in the battle at Bunker Hill. The bravery and ferocity displayed by the Americans at Bunker Hill quickly became the stuff of legend, and the fallen patriots were instantly hailed as martyrs. Reports from the field reported that Warren, befitting his position as a major general, was one of the last defenders to retreat from the British attack, before being shot in the head. Within months, as the tale of the battle at Bunker Hill spread through the colonies, Warren was elevated to a special status as "first martyr to the cause of American liberty."[29]

Following the lead of Bostonians like Hancock and Warren, leaders throughout the colonies began to champion the revolutionary cause by tapping this ancient spiritual inheritance and framing it in new terms. More and more, the term "patriot" served as a functional equivalent for "martyr" in the American vernacular. As a self-proclaimed "Patriot Poet" declared in a September 12, 1775, issue of the *New Hampshire Gazette*:

What! Can those British Tyrants think
Our Fathers cross'd the main;
And savage Foes and Dangers met,
To be enslav'd by them?
If so, they are mistaken
For we will rather die;
And since they have become our Foes,
Their Forces we defy.
And all the world shall know,
Americans are free;
Nor slaves nor cowards we will prove—
Great Britain soon shall see.[30]

The time was nearing, this upstart generation began to declare, when true patriots would be called to offer themselves in self-sacrifice to the American cause.

In this way, the tradition of English Protestant martyrdom was deeply linked to the colonists' emerging national identity. To be a "true American" was to be willing to die for the revolutionary cause, and to die for the revolutionary cause was to earn a ticket to paradise. As Hancock put it in his 1774 speech commemorating the Boston Massacre, "'tis immortality to sacrifice ourselves for the salvation of our country. We fear not death."[31]

This link between the revolutionary war, the Christian religion, and an emerging American nationalism was formalized with the embrace of Protestant chaplains to the Continental Congresses and the Continental Army. Chaplains to the Continental Congress opened the sessions with prayer, presided over traditional observances like fast days and Christian holidays, and preached on special occasions. A key objective of these sermons was to help members of Congress who heard them—and members of the public who would read them afterward—to see themselves as connected to the revolution as a sacred cause. Even those who did not die on the fields of battle could be true patriots.

In a sermon entitled *Death, the Last Enemy*, Samuel Stillman eulogized Samuel Ward, the Rhode Island delegate to the Continental Congress, who succumbed to smallpox in Philadelphia on March 26, 1776. Preaching the next day to the assembled Congress, Stillman connected Ward to Joseph Warren, the leading Massachusetts revolutionary who was among the casualties in the first formal battles of the War of Independence, the battles of Lexington and Concord. Calling Warren "that Proto-Martyr to the Liberties of America," Stillman then hailed Peyton Randolph, the first president of the Continental Congress, who had died in October of the previous year. Conjuring a long lineage of Protestant martyrs, Stillman concluded by assuring the members of their Congress of Ward's comportment in his final days, a sure sign of his eternal fate: "In his last illness he appeared composed, having placed his expectation of eternal merits of Jesus Christ . . . his immortal part hath joined the spirits of just men made perfect, who continually surround the throne of God."[32]

Protestant chaplains in the Continental Army likewise routinely portrayed the American cause as a holy war, and so they encouraged American soldiers to embrace martyrdom as the proper frame for understanding their prospective deaths. As Abiel Leonard, chaplain to the Continental Army, put it in *A prayer, composed for the benefit of the soldiery, in the American army, to assist them in their private devotions*:

> Teach, I pray thee, my hands to war, and my fingers to fight in the defence of America, and the rights and liberties of it! Impress upon my mind a true sense of my duty, and the obligation I am under to my country! And enable me to pay a due and respect to all my officers. Grant unto me a courage, zeal and resolution in the day of battle, that I may play the man for my people, and the cities of my God; chusing rather to lay down my life, than either through cowardice or desertion betray the glorious cause I am engaged in.[33]

While addressing troops under the command of General Arthur St. Clair in October 1776, another chaplain summed things up by declaring, quite simply, that any soldier who might fall in the revolutionary cause "will be justly esteemed a Martyr to liberty."[34]

Indeed, countless young soldiers in George Washington's Continental Army were steeped in the ideals of martyrdom from the time they learned to read *The New England Primer*. Just one idiomatic expression of this tradition, for instance—the encouragement to "play the man"—was pervasive in colonial literature. It could be found in the King James Version of the Bible and in countless accounts in John Foxe's *Book of Martyrs*. It could be found in the climactic scene of John Bunyan's classic, *Pilgrim's Progress*. It could be found in any of dozens of "muster sermons" printed in Boston in the decades leading up to the Revolutionary War.[35] It could be found in captivity narratives, newspapers, and almanacs that circulated widely throughout the War of Independence.[36] It could be found in John Hancock's 1774 speech commemorating the Boston Massacre and Abiel Leonard's prayer for the Continental Army.

Or consider the expression attributed in American lore to the revolutionary spy, Nathan Hale: "I regret that I have but one life to lose for my country." After responding to George Washington's appeal for a volunteer, Hale entered British-occupied New York on September 17. He was captured on September 21, 1776, and executed the next day by British troops under the command of General William Howe. He was twenty-one years old.[37] Whether or not he said them before his execution, there is little doubt that Hale was familiar with the words that were attached to him in memory. So was almost every soldier under George Washington's direct command, because Washington made sure that his charges were familiar with the play from which the lines were drawn, Addison's *Cato*. Washington encouraged his troops to stage the play for entertainment, edification, and inspiration between battles, including its climactic scene in which the title character bravely confronts his death, declaring, "How beautiful is death when earned by virtue. Who would not be that youth? What pity it is that we can die but once to serve our country!"[38] Young men who played the part successfully were heralded by others for "making an Excellent Die."[39]

It was not just printers and preachers and soldiers, however, who evoked the tradition of English Protestant martyrdom as they committed themselves to the cause of American Independence. The evocative and passionate language born from this tradition could be heard in countless patriot rallying cries, from the cry that became associated with Patrick Henry, "Give me liberty or give me death," to the slogan that would become the New Hampshire state slogan, "Live Free or Die." George Washington himself heralded the virtues of martyrdom in his General Orders to the Continental Army on July 2, 1776, the same day his colleagues in the Continental Congress voted for independence: "Our cruel and unrelenting Enemy leaves us no choice but a brave resistance, or the most abject submission; this is all we can expect—We have therefore to resolve to conquer or die: Our own Country's Honor, all call upon us for a vigorous and manly exertion."[40]

Evocative, spiritual language like this was not ethereal or incidental or inconsequential. It can be found at every turn in the historical record for generations leading up to the War of Independence. It was discourse shared by Virginians like Washington, Jefferson, and Henry; by New Englanders like John Adams, Samuel Adams, Paul Revere, Joseph Warren, and John Hancock; and by Pennsylvanians like Benjamin Franklin and John Dickinson. All embraced the inherited tradition of English Protestant martyrdom and adapted it readily to the cause of the American Revolution. Their calls for vigilance and continual self-sacrifice continued even after the Revolutionary

War was concluded. As Jefferson wrote to his friend William Stephens Smith in 1787, "The tree of liberty must be refreshed from time to time with the blood of patriots and tyrants."

In this sense it is indisputable that the Christian religion played an indispensable role in the founding of the United States. But the kind of Christianity on which the nation was founded was a public religion of war, grounded in the ancient tradition of English Protestant martyrdom. From the root of this spiritual inheritance springs American patriotism, what John Hancock called "this most noble sentiment." From this same root springs white Christian nationalism, an American heresy.

Patriotism and Nationalism

As did their Protestant forebears, English colonists in North America associated true Christian faith with demonstrations of virtue, as exemplified by the ideal of martyrdom. Young boys, especially, were taught to expect that someday they might be called to fight and die for a sacred cause and that should this come to pass, their deaths could be meaningful in the eyes of others and meaningful in the eyes of God. Young men were encouraged to aspire to this idealized vision of masculine virtue as part of their coming of age. In pulpits across the colonies, and as chaplains to colonial militia, English clergy in the colonies blessed generations of soldiers who fought in wars against England's colonial competitors, the French and the Spanish. Along the way, they also blessed generations of predatory violence against the Native peoples of North America.

The ideal of dying a self-sacrificing death for a sacred cause inspired early English colonists to prepare themselves diligently, so that they would be prepared should destiny call upon them to "play the man." They passed these beliefs and practices down from generation to generation, where they were widely embraced by leaders of the American Revolution, by Protestant chaplains to the Continental Congresses and Continental Army, and by rank-and-file soldiers under the command of George Washington. Protestant clergy, printers, songwriters, and pamphleteers from across the colonies adapted the spirit of English Protestant martyrdom to the new circumstances of the American Revolution. Often, these first American nationalists simply called it patriotism.

Leading revolutionaries often justified their cause by using multivalent words like "liberty" and "tyranny," "virtue" and "corruption." Many historians of the American Revolution characterize this vocabulary as "political" and associate it with John Locke, whose writings were so popular among revolutionary elite. But this vocabulary can just as easily be traced to John Foxe's *Book of Martyrs*, the landmark sixteenth-century compendium of English Protestant martyrdom. So, too, can additional language that is pervasive in the historical record but often overlooked by historians—language like "sacrifice" and "immortality" and "playing the man." Those unfamiliar with this intrinsically religious field of meaning end up painting entirely partial pictures of the origins of the American Revolution.

White Protestant American culture remains deeply rooted in this veneration of self-sacrifice as the supreme expression of especially masculine virtue. This passionate Protestantism can inspire genuine passion and honorable conduct—a strong sense of right and wrong, a willingness to sacrifice for something greater than oneself, a devotion to a cause that can find expression in demonstrations of great courage and valor. Inherently oppositional, it finds its fullest expression of virtue in "the good fight." Millions of Americans attach this spirit to their love of country, and it plays an indispensable role in cultivating a powerful sense of American national identity, as can be attested by anyone who has ever stood for the national anthem at a professional sporting event.[41]

The dark side of this Protestant commitment to the principle of virtue stems from its starkly dualistic worldview. People who surrender to the darker side of this tradition can reduce almost any conflict to a battle of good versus evil. This spiritual surrender renders people prone to absolutism and to the belief that the truest sign of righteousness is always and everywhere confrontation. It can easily culminate in political extremism, often associated with a toxic brand of masculinity that sees almost any conflict as requiring the exercise of violence. This dysfunctional and damaging way of orienting to conflict is a bitter fruit that also springs from the Protestant roots of the American founding. True men (from the Latin *vir* for man, root of both "virile" and "virtue") are those who will "man up" and die for the sacred cause. For some this yearning is so deep that if no cause is readily accessible, they will invent one.

Across the expanse of American history, this spirit has been made manifest in an enormous range of ways, from the virulent racism of white supremacists to the radicalism of the early abolitionists, from the veneration that most Americans hold for those who serve in the US armed forces, to the fervent pacifism of those who have protested American wars. These diverse expressions can all be traced to the oppositional spirit of early English Protestantism and to the ideals of martyrdom that were intrinsic to the passionate American brand of Protestantism in which America's revolutionary generations were so deeply steeped.

This distinctively American predisposition to dramatic demonstrations of self-sacrifice is a cornerstone of "white Christian nationalism." This ideology invites distorted expressions of American virtue, a kind of idealistic American patriotism gone terribly, terribly wrong. As with any other deep social dysfunction, white Christian nationalism often flourishes in the fertile soil of lives shaped by multigenerational dysfunction and trauma.[42] But whatever its social and psychological roots,

many who embrace it understand Protestant virtue to sanction the complete fusion of national and religious devotion—
what Philip Gorski and Samuel Perry call "The Flag and
the Cross." As Greg Locke, pastor of the Global Vision Bible
Church in Wilson County, Tennessee, proclaimed at the rally
in Washington on January 5, 2021, the night before the insurrection, "Lord, we've gotta recognize the fact if we don't have
convictions worth dying for, we don't even know what living
really is. So, God, help us to live, help us to fight, and if need
be, lay down our life for this nation, and we thank you for those
that have gone before us and done just that."[43] Declarations like
this may sound forth from the lips of the virtuous as the height
of patriotism. From the lips of people enthralled by violence,
consumed by nostalgia, seduced by racism, susceptible to
propaganda, and prone to conspiratorial thinking, these declarations are easy to recognize as crystalline expressions of white
Christian nationalism. They are easy to recognize as American
heresy.

The day after Greg Locke preached that message, several
thousand people, spearheaded by the Proud Boys and Oath
Keepers, laid violent siege to the US Capitol. Like millions
of other Americans, I watched those events unfold on televi-
sion, stunned in a way I hadn't felt stunned since watching the
terrorist attacks of September 11, 2001. It occurred to me then
that "January 6" would become a date that would no longer
require mention of a year for people to know what events were
being talked about. Like "9/11," there will forever be only one
"January 6" in American history. The date has become what
Franklin Delano Roosevelt called December 7, 1941, the day
that Japanese fighter pilots bombed Pearl Harbor, "a day that
will live in infamy."

But millions of Americans celebrated what happened that
day—applauding the men who stormed the Capitol and afterward hailing Ashli Babbitt, the San Diego woman killed by

Capitol Police that day. In the years since, Babbitt has been elevated to the status of legend on the American Right, where she is widely portrayed as a martyr to a noble cause.[44] As have their forebears for generations, many Americans today take for granted that the agents of evil in the world will continue to mount threats routinely and ongoingly to the truth. These Americans expect these threats to come not just from outside the American body politic but also from within the institutions of government at every level. In their view, meeting these threats requires the exercise of bravado and virtue, up to and including the exercise of violence. Come what may, win or lose, the truly faithful must remain ever vigilant. At a moment's notice, true Americans may be required to man up and fight.

Not long after January 6, a friend and his wife came to visit in San Diego. My friend and I have sustained a great relationship across many years, even knowing how differently we think about some things, politics among them. I have always admired him and his wife for the way they took care of his mother as she struggled mightily through the last years of her life. Their care for her was extraordinary, a true demonstration of self-sacrifice. Now it is my turn to take care of my aging parents. At almost ninety, my parents, too, are failing, and I am struggling to care for them, burdened more by the sadness than by the tasks that their care requires of me. I wonder sometimes whether I am rising to the challenge that my friend met, the challenge that the gospel of John suggests that Jesus gave to his disciples: "This is my commandment, That ye love one another, as I have loved you. Greater love hath no man than this, that a man lay down his life for his friends."

One sunny afternoon, my friend and I had a few hours to ourselves. I chose to take him to Cabrillo National Monument, a site at the tip of San Diego's Point Loma Peninsula, looking out on the expansive Pacific Ocean. I knew my friend would enjoy this site. He joined the navy out of high school and served on a nuclear submarine, training that set him on the course for a career in the nuclear energy industry. We got to the National Monument as the gates were closing, though, and so chose instead to drive through the adjacent Fort Rosecrans National Cemetery, which also sports spectacular ocean views. We drove through row upon row of headstones, most with crosses, a few with stars of David, some with no religious symbol at all. A huge swath of the cemetery was home to tombstones dated with deaths between 1940 and 1945, the years of World War II. We drove mostly in silence, until my friend said, "Kind of humbling, isn't it?" I agreed entirely that it was.

Long Reach

To ask, "was the United States founded as a Christian nation?" is to ask the wrong question.

In formal and institutional terms, the answer to the question is clearly "no." At the time of the American Revolution, the religious landscape varied enormously across the thirteen participating colonies. Protecting religious liberty was at the forefront of the revolutionaries' concerns. It is no coincidence that there is no national church in the United States, nor that the framers of the US Constitution explicitly prohibited religious tests for public office. For many who fought in it, the Revolutionary War was a struggle for independence from the twin powers of the English Crown *and the Church of England.* The founders of the United States clearly understood the religious liberties they were fighting for to extend beyond the Christian faith.[1] After the Hebrew Congregations of Philadelphia, New York, Charleston, and Richmond sent their joint congratulations to George Washington for his inauguration as the first US president in 1789; Washington responded in writing, beginning with this declaration: "The liberality of sentiment toward each other which marks every political and religious denomination of men in this Country, stands unparalleled in the history of Nations."

It is equally clear, however, that the founders did not draw sharp distinctions between the sacred and secular spheres of life, even as they secured the separation of church and state as a central plank in the platform of the American Revolution.

As Washington wrote in the same letter to the Hebrew leaders, "The Power and Goodness of the Almighty were strongly Manifested in the events of our late glorious revolution; and his kind interposition in our behalf has been no less visible in the establishment of our present equal government. In war he directed the Sword; and in peace he has ruled in our Councils."[2]

This way of thinking can be difficult for modern Americans to comprehend. Some, upon reading Washington extol the separation of church and state, might imagine him as an enlightened figure, committed to transcending the conservative Anglicanism of his native Virginia. Some, upon reading Washington sing the praises of "Almighty" God, might suspect him to be an evangelical Christian intent on spreading his religious views. Both would be wrong. George Washington was committed entirely to the separation of church and state and spoke rarely of his own personal faith in public. He also believed that both his life and the life of the new nation he helped to found were governed indelibly by the God portrayed in the Christian Bible. His views do not conform to those of either the contemporary secular Left or the conservative religious Right.

In Mark Noll's estimation, the late eighteenth century marked the beginning of an epochal transition away from the assumption that "all spheres of life are intertwined" and toward "the distinguishing of the realms of religion and everything else."[3] But signs of this transition are scarce in the writings of even among the most educated of the revolutionary elite. As Robert Middlekauff summed things up in his 2005 *The Glorious Cause*, the American revolutionaries were at once committed to political ideals of liberty and representative government, and at the same time they were "marked by the moral dispositions of a passionate Protestantism." Of this latter inheritance, Middlekauff wrote:

They could not escape this culture; nor did they try. They were imbued with an American moralism that colored all

their perceptions of politics . . . [they] believed that they had
been selected by Providence to do great deeds. They had been
chosen, and their victory in the war and the achievement of
independence demonstrated the worth of their calling.[4]

Attempting to describe this mindset to modern readers,
Middlekauff labeled the revolutionaries "children of the
twice-born."

To understand the revolutionaries in full dimension, then,
we must accept that their aspirations were shaped by more than
what today we comfortably characterize as secular concerns. We
must take them on their own terms, which means taking them
seriously as religious, as well as political and economic, actors.
The revolutionary movement was inherently, intrinsically, both
religious and political at the same time, and successive generations of Americans institutionalized and memorialized the
Revolution as the fulfillment of this double destiny.

Instead of asking, "Was the US founded as a Christian
nation?" it is more important to ask, "What role did religion
play in the founding of the United States?" And even more
critical is the necessary follow-up: "And what kind of religion
was it?" These questions broaden the field of inquiry beyond
the formal and institutional, challenging us to consider the
cultural and spiritual inheritance that the founders bequeathed
to their descendants, the people called "Americans."

In response to this line of inquiry, most students of American
history will rightly think of the "natural law tradition," which
leading revolutionaries conjured so frequently by invoking the
writings of John Locke. But this tradition was by no means the
dominant religious view in revolutionary America, and even
those who embraced it did not understand themselves in doing
so to be abandoning a larger stream of Christian thought and
practice that prevailed among their peers. This larger stream
was early English Protestantism, several branches of which
had been transplanted by English colonists in North America
across the seventeenth and early eighteenth centuries. Through

the middle decades of the eighteenth century, leading colonists found ways to forge bonds of solidarity across these many branches. The result was the flowering of a new Protestant vernacular that in many ways amounted to its own religious tradition. This American brand of early English Protestantism was fundamentally oppositional. It encouraged the devout to think of the life of faith as a perpetual spiritual battle, over and against an array of dark and sinister forces conspiring to extinguish American—which was to say Protestant—liberty. It took pride in fighting the good fight and considered dying for a sacred cause the very pinnacle of human achievement. It was rooted in a sense of providential destiny that encouraged many, perhaps most, to think of "American" as a religious and ethnic, as well as nationalist, identity.

In short, the American founding stemmed as much from the worldview of John Foxe, the early English martyrologist, as it did from the worldview of John Locke. The founders of the United States bequeathed this spiritual inheritance to their descendants—and to all of us who call ourselves white and American.

In a prior book, born from my curiosity about the revolutionary martyr Nathan Hale, I described this spiritual inheritance, in moral and spiritual terms, as a double-edged sword. On the one hand, it can inspire a profound sense of purpose and destiny, imbued with the dimension of the divine, rendering us capable of extraordinary sacrifice for causes greater than ourselves. This same inheritance, however, predisposes us to absolutize our every conflict and to demonize our every perceived enemy.

In this book I have used a different metaphor: the religious roots of the American experiment run deep, and their reach extends powerfully into our present life as a nation. From these religious roots still spring both sweet and bitter fruits. The sweet fruits—order, purpose, progress, innovation, liberty, and patriotism—are widely available and rightly celebrated in the United States today. Despite the fact that these fruits are not distributed fairly or shared equally, people from around the world still come to the United States in search of them, and many find them far more plentiful here than they were in the lands from which they came. But the bitter fruits—violence, nostalgia, racism, propaganda, conspiratorial thinking, and nationalism—also remain powerfully present in our public life. They continue to feed the demon that is white Christian nationalism, a Christian heresy.

How can we best resist the temptations that this heresy presents? I have tried to hint at answers to this question throughout this book, while keeping in mind white Americans occupying three different religious or ideological positions. Now I share a word of challenge and invitation to each.

Too many secular Americans succumb to the temptation of denying or dismissing as inconsequential the religious roots of the American founding. Secular Americans who embrace this attitude will continue to overlook—and therefore to misunderstand—some of the essential dynamics of the American past and present. To describe the American founding as partly religious in nature is not to seek the undoing of constitutional protections, nor the whitewashing of Christian complicity in the systemic evils of genocide, racism, patriarchy, and the like. It is to acknowledge that the motivations of those who led the American Revolution cannot be reduced to narrow political and economic concerns. It is to acknowledge that there are spiritual ("ideological," if you must) dimensions to American culture that are derived from the Protestant inheritance shared by the large majority of those who fought in the War of Independence and who established the institutions of the new nation. As I have tried to make clear, I view this inheritance as the source of both sweet and bitter fruit—in religious language, the source of both blessing and curse. I invite secular and non-Christian Americans interested in combatting white Christian nationalism to engage more deeply with religious Americans, especially those who may—by virtue of their religious formation and perspective—provide a deeper and better insight into the nature of the disease.

Conservative religious Americans must learn to embrace the emerging conversation about white Christian nationalism as more than cultural condescension. Rod Martin, one of the founders of the Conservative Baptist Network, caricatured the conversation this way when speaking to a friendly audience in 2021: "Let's demonize patriotism by calling it nationalism and associating that with Hitler. Ah, now let's call it white nationalism. . . . Then we'll call it Christian nationalist so we'll make it sound like you are the ayatollah. It is all designed to demonize you."[5] But defensiveness like this misrepresents the case that more and more white Christians are putting forth. To say, as I have in this book, that the founders of the United States succumbed to the temptations of this American heresy is not to dismiss them, individually, as mere "heretics." It is to take them down off their pedestals, though, and to consider them in full dimension, subject to all the frailties of the human condition. It is to acknowledge that George Washington was a heroic military leader, a statesmanlike politician, *and* a predatory land speculator. It is to acknowledge that Thomas Jefferson was a literary genius, an outspoken champion of Enlightenment ideals, *and* a man bewitched by deeply racist views of American "Negroes," including those he considered his own property and including among those even the woman he took as a concubine and his own children by her. It is to acknowledge that Benjamin Franklin was an unparalleled entrepreneur, a scientific visionary, *and* a mass media profiteer. It is to acknowledge that Joseph Warren was an inspiring orator, a heroic first martyr to the cause of the American Revolution, *and* an apologist for genocide. It is to acknowledge that Samuel Adams was an extraordinary organizer, a peerless spokesperson for the revolutionary cause, *and* a conspiracy theorist. It is to acknowledge that young men like Nathan Hale were loyal revolutionary soldiers, exemplars of Christian faith, *and* enthralled with the idea of martyrdom. And so on. I applaud those conservative Christian Americans who are willing to set aside the lenses of romance and nostalgia in considering the complex American past. Those willing to do so can play an indispensable role in creating a better future for our nation.

Finally, then, I extend a word of challenge and invitation to people from my own spiritual tribe, the people who think of ourselves as white and Christian and progressive. Too many of us seem determined to exempt ourselves from self-examination. It is right and good to identify with the liberating and justice-seeking streams of the Christian tradition. But we are kidding ourselves if we think our lives are carried only in these streams. Owing to our spiritual inheritance, all of us who call ourselves white and Christian and American are habituated to ways of thought and practice that betray our Christian faith. We, too, are susceptible to the temptations of white Christian nationalism. In recent years, a moral awakening has swept the American Left on matters pertaining to white racism. A similar awakening is needed on matters relating to white religion, and progressive white Christians have a critical role to play. The role, however, may not be the one to which we are accustomed. In addition to standing on the front lines of social justice, we may also be advised to kneel on the front pews of repentance. If we pray sincerely, "Lord have mercy, Lord have mercy upon us," perhaps others will join us. I have tried to write this book in this spirit, hoping that someday we who are white and Christian and American will rise together from our knees and stand prepared to offer the sweetest of all fruit, the fruit described in the gospel of Matthew as "fruit meet for repentance" (Matthew 3:8, KJV).

Notes

Introduction

1 Ibram X. Kendi, *Stamped from the Beginning: The Definitive History of Racist Ideas in America* (New York: Perseus Books, 2016). Nikole Hannah-Jones, *The 1619 Project: A New Origin Story* (New York: One World, 2021). See also https://1619books.com/.

2 Elizabeth Dias and Ruth Graham, "The Growing Religious Fervor in the American Right: 'This Is a Jesus Movement,'" *New York Times*, April 6, 2022, https://tinyurl.com/38zzwpjh.

3 Peter Manseau, "Christmas Cards with Guns Reflect Muscular Christianity, with Its 'Virile and Manly' Jesus," *Washington Post*, December 14, 2021, https://tinyurl.com/4wvajcdk.

4 Philip S. Gorski and Samuel L. Perry, *The Flag and the Cross: White Christian Nationalism and the Threat to American Democracy* (New York: Oxford University Press), 4–5.

5 For an excellent elaboration of this point, see Robert P. Jones, *White Too Long: The Legacy of White Supremacy in American Christianity* (New York: Simon & Schuster, 2020), 9. What Jones says about "white supremacy" is equally true of white Christian nationalism: its "norms . . . have become deeply and broadly integrated into white Christian identity, operating far below the level of consciousness."

6 See Christians against Christian Nationalism, accessed February 8, 2023, www.christiansagainstchristiannationalism.org.

7 Pierre L. van den Berghe, *Race and Racism: A Comparative Perspective* (New York: Wiley, 1967), 78. For a good summary of van den Berghe's argument see Justin C. Mueller, "America's Herrenvolk Democracy Is a Social Democracy for the White Majority," *Milwaukee Independent*, November 3, 2017.

8 For recent contributions to this conversation, now underway for a generation, see Kendi's *Stamped from the Beginning*, Hannah-Jones's *The 1619 Project*, and Woody Holton, *Liberty Is Sweet: The Hidden History of the American Revolution* (New York: Simon & Schuster, 2021).

9 For a sample of their work, see: Philip Gorksi, *American Babylon: Christianity and Democracy before and after Trump* (London and New York: Routledge, 2020); Andrew Whitehead and Samuel Perry, *Taking America Back for God: Christian Nationalism in the United States* (New York: Oxford University Press, 2020); Kristin Kobes Du Mez, *Jesus and John Wayne: How White Evangelicals Corrupted a Faith and Fractured a Nation* (New York: Liveright Publishing, 2020); R. Marie Griffith, *Moral Combat: How Sex Divided American Christians and Fractured American Politics* (New York: Basic Books, 2017); Randall Balmer, *Bad Faith: Race and the Rise of the Religious Right* (Grand Rapids, MI: Eerdmans, 2021); Bradley Onishi, *Preparing for War: The Extremist History of White Christian Nationalism—and What Comes Next* (Minneapolis: Broadleaf Books, 2023); Jemar Tisby, *The Color of Compromise: The Truth about the American Church's Complicity in Racism* (Grand Rapids, MI: Zondervan, 2017).

10 See Christians against Christian Nationalism, "Statement," accessed February 14, 2023, https://tinyurl.com/yckhdxa8.

Chapter 1

1 The *Oxford English Dictionary* (1933) defines the Common Law as "The unwritten law of England, administered by the King's courts, which purports to be derived from ancient usage."

2 See John Cotton, *God's Promise to His Plantation* (1630), American Literature Anthology Project, accessed March 15, 2023, https://tinyurl.com/2uesszud. To the first of his ways, Cotton added the following qualification: "But this course of warring against others, & driving them out without provocation, depends upon speciall Commission from God, or else it is not imitable."

3 As Bernard Bailyn summarized in his landmark 1967 *The Ideological Origins of the American Revolution*, "In pamphlet after pamphlet, the Americans cited Locke on natural rights and on the social and governmental contract . . . [often] in the most offhand way." (Cambridge, MA: Belknap Press of Harvard University Press, 1967), 27–28.

4 Justin Dyer, "Is America a Christian Nation? Yes and No," *Washington Post*, January 3, 2023, https://tinyurl.com/2frkv8un.

5 John Locke, *Two Treatises of Government* (London: A. Millar, 1764), 54, 132. Locke continued: "Whatsoever then he removes out of the state that nature hath provided, and left it in, he hath mixed his labour with, and joined to it something that is his own, and thereby makes it his property. As much land as a man tills, plants, improves, cultivates, and can use the product of, so much is his property. He by his labour does, as it were, inclose it from the common. It being by him removed from the common state nature hath placed it in, it hath by this labour something annexed to it, that excludes the common right of other men. For this labour being the unquestionable property of the labourer, no man but he can have a right to what that is once joined to, at least where there is enough, and as good, left in common for others."

6 Ed Dolan, "Taking Locke Seriously: Of Government, Property Rights, and Climate Change," Niskanen Center, December 10, 2020, https://tinyurl.com/4azxubuw. "These rights and duties were reflected in the English common law of Locke's day. Violation of the duty not to harm others in their persons corresponds to the common law torts of assault (threatening or attempting to inflict offensive physical contact) and battery (carrying out a threat to harm). Violation of the second duty, when it pertains to personal property, is theft. Interference with others' use of their land by knowingly entering it without permission is the common law offense of trespass. Actual harm is not an essential element of trespass—any interference with the owner's right to exclusive possession and enjoyment of property qualifies."

7 Locke, *Two Treatises*, 105.

8 Kathryn Gin Lum, *Heathen: Religion and Race in American History* (Cambridge, MA: Harvard University Press, 2022), 28.

9 William Cronon, *Changes in the Land: Indians, Colonists, and the Ecology of New England* (New York: Hill & Wang, 1983), 55. Cronon elaborates: "A people who moved so much and worked so little did not deserve to lay claim to the land they inhabited. Their supposed failure to 'improve' that land was a token not of their chosen way of life but of their laziness."

10 William Jewell, *The Golden Cabinet of True Treasure* (London: John Crosley, 1612; Ann Arbor: Text Creation Partnership, 2011), chap. 8, 167.

11 Neal Salisbury, ed., *The Sovereignty and Goodness of God, by Mary Rowlandson, with Related Documents* (Boston and New York: Bedford/St. Martin's, 1997), 19.

12 Cotton Mather, *Just Commemorations: The Death of Good Men, Considered* (Boston: Bartholomew Green, 1715), 48–52.

13 Lum, *Heathen*, 43.

14 John W. Shy, *A People Numerous and Armed: Reflections on the Military Struggle for American Independence* (Ann Arbor: University of Michigan Press, 1990), 123. See also Sarah J. Purcell, *Sealed with Blood: War, Sacrifice, and Memory in Revolutionary America* (Philadelphia: University of Pennsylvania University Press, 2002), 123.

15 This will be detailed in chapter 3. See chapter 3, note 23.

16 The quote is from the elder Richard Hakluyt; Peter C. Mancall, *Hakluyt's Promise: An Elizabethan's Obsession for English America* (New Haven, CT: Yale University Press, 2007), 164.

17 The English Crown, "First Charter of Virginia (1606)," *Encyclopedia Virginia*, accessed March 15, 2023, https://tinyurl.com/36u62at5.

18 Annette Gordon-Reed, *The Hemingses of Monticello* (New York: W. W. Norton, 2008), 40.

19 See Holton, *Liberty Is Sweet*, 5.

20 According to Holton, all this "set the stage for the American Revolution" more so than the mere taxation of the colonies. "British officials and American colonists came out of it with conflicting ideas about Indians." Holton, *Liberty Is Sweet*, 14ff.

21 Shy, *A People Numerous and Armed*, 293.

22 Mark Fisher and Josh Keller, "Why Does the US Have so Many Mass Shootings? Research Is Clear: Guns," *New York Times*, November 7, 2017, https://tinyurl.com/3b5z27wt.

23 "Sanford Men Accused of Damaging Teen's Car in Confrontation over Speeding," YouTube, accessed February 8, 2023, https://tinyurl.com/yc7u6h7p.

24 Keeanga-Yamahtta Taylor, "American Racism and the Buffalo Shooting," *The New Yorker*, May 15, 2022, https://tinyurl.com/y4tewmyy.

25 The quote is from William Darity's interview with NPR: "'From Here to Equality' Author Makes a Case, and a Plan, for Reparations," NPR, June 17, 2020, https://tinyurl.com/yc6yb3yj. See also William A. Darity Jr. and A. Kirsten Mullen, *From Here to Equality: Reparations for Black Americans in the Twenty-First Century* (Chapel Hill: University of North Carolina Press, 2020).

26 Farrell Evans, "How Interstate Highways Gutted Communities—and Reinforced Segregation," HISTORY, October 20, 2021, https://tinyurl.com/y6973rwc.

27 Eylul Tekin, "Exploring Racial Discrimination in Mortgage Lending: A Call for Greater Transparency," Clever Real Estate, updated February 6, 2023, https://tinyurl.com/2wd5hafk.

Chapter 2

1   Ismat Sarah Mangla, "More Than Half of Americans Believe God Granted the US a Special Role in Human History," businessinsider.com, June 24, 2015, https://tinyurl.com/3r73ub8r.

2   First produced in 1549 under King Edward VI, the collection of prayer books that would come to be known as the "Common Prayer" had undergone a substantial revision in the aftermath of the English Civil War (1642–51). The resulting version of 1662 proved so satisfactory that it was not revised until 1789, and thus represents the edition that would have been widely available in North America through the period of the American Revolution.

3   John Flavel, *The Mystery of Providence* (West Linn, OR: Monergism Books, 2018), 1.

4   Glenda Goodman, "'The Tears I Shed at the Songs of Thy Church': Seventeenth-Century Musical Piety in the English Atlantic World," *Journal of the American Musicological Society* 65, no. 3 (2012): 691–725. According to Goodman (692), "Puritans believed psalmody created a channel between the singer and God: by singing, the devout glorified and praised God, but, through singing, the worshiper was also brought closer to the divine. The soul was lifted."

5   William T. Dargan, *Lining Out the Word: Dr. Watts Hymn Singing in the Music of Black Americans* (Berkeley: University of California Press, 2006), 94.

6   Isaac Watts, *Divine Songs Attempted in Easy Language for the Use of Children . . . Seventh Edition* (Boston: Kneeland & Green for Henchman, 1730), 2–3.

7   For more on this see Erik Routley, *Christian Hymns Observed: When in Our Music God Is Glorified* (Princeton, NJ: Prestige Publications, 1982).

8   *Bradford's History of Plymouth Plantation, 1606–1646*, ed. William T. Davis (New York: Charles Scribner's Sons, 1908), 124, https://tinyurl.com/ynjfhtu5.

9   Quoted in George B. Cheever, *The Journal of the Pilgrims at Plymouth* (New York: John Wiley, 1849), 143.

10 For more on this see Salisbury, *The Sovereignty and Goodness of God* and John Demos, *The Unredeemed Captive* (New York: Random House, 1995).

11 Samuel Danforth, *A Brief Recognition of New England's Errand into the Wilderness* (Cambridge, MA: Samuel Green, 1671).

12 George McKenna, *The Puritan Origins of American Patriotism* (New Haven, CT: Yale University Press, 2007), 50.

13　Robert G. Parkinson, *The Common Cause: Creating Race and Nation in the American Revolution* (Chapel Hill: University of North Carolina Press, 2016), loc. 324 of 17188, Kindle.

14　Samuel Bird, *The Importance of the Divine Presence* (New Haven, CT: James Parker, 1759), 4.

15　Thomas S. Kidd, *God of Liberty: A Religious History of the American Revolution* (New York: Basic Books, 2010), 9.

16　James Allen, *The Poem Which The Committee . . .* (Boston: E. Russell, 1772), 7.

17　Joseph Warren, *An Oration; Delivered March the 6th, 1775* (New York: 1775), 3, 5.

18　"First Prayer of the Continental Congress, 1774," Office of the Chaplain, United States House of Representatives, accessed February 8, 2023, https://tinyurl.com/2p95ncc7.

19　*Congressional Proclamation, June 12, 1775* (Philadelphia: William & Thomas Bradford, 1775).

20　Daniel Batwell, *A Sermon Preached at York-Town* (Philadelphia: Dunlap, 1775), 17–20.

21　"Benjamin Franklin's Great Seal Design," GreatSeal.com, accessed February 8, 2023, https://tinyurl.com/3c9ssv9y.

22　"America (My Country, 'Tis of Thee)," Wikipedia, accessed February 8, 2023, https://tinyurl.com/4unenapv.

23　David W. Blight, *Race and Reunion: The Civil War in American Memory* (Cambridge, MA: Harvard University Press, 2001), 189.

24　Taylor, "American Racism and the Buffalo Shooting."

25　For instance, in a December 17, 2022, email entitled "Do Our Young People Understand This?," Larry P. Arn, the president of the conservative online Hillsdale College, wrote to supporters, "It is a simple fact that the way our government operates has been radically transformed since the 1960s. Key to this transformation was the undermining of intelligent patriotism among younger Americans by promoting a **false** and **dishonest** account of America's history in our schools and universities."

26　"Lincoln on America, December 1, 1862: Closing Paragraph in Message to Congress," National Park Service, accessed February 8, 2023, https://tinyurl.com/ycknfs5b.

27　On the Lost Cause, see Charles Reagan Wilson, *Baptized in Blood: The Religion of the Lost Cause* (Athens: University of Georgia Press, 1983), https://tinyurl.com/455jxvva. On the KKK, see Kelly J. Baker, "Religion and the Rise of the Second Ku Klux Klan," *Readex* 4, no. 3 (September 2009), https://tinyurl.com/jku9fj44. On the Progressive Movement, see Marta Cook and John Halpin, "The Role of Faith in the Progressive Movement," AmericanProgress.org, October 8,

2010, https://tinyurl.com/wbs7x7uw. On the Social Gospel, see *The Editors of the Encyclopaedia Britannica*, "Walter Rauschenbusch," *Encyclopaedia Britannica*, accessed February 8, 2023, https://tinyurl.com/rfcyp447. On MLK Jr.'s dream, see "I Have a Dream," AmericanRhetoric.com, accessed February 8, 2023, https://tinyurl.com/5n6fbtrm.

28   "MLK's 'content of character' quote inspires debate," CBS News, January 20, 2013, https://tinyurl.com/35y8wjtm.

29   In a February 8, 1958, article written for *The Gospel Messenger*, the official periodical of the Church of the Brethren, King deployed the saying in quotation marks, paraphrasing a statement first made by a nineteenth-century Unitarian minister, Theodore Parker. He did so, though, by placing it in the context of "The deep rumblings of discontent from Asia and Africa" that "are at bottom a quest for freedom and human dignity on the part of people who have long been the victims of colonialism and imperialism." The reason the arc of the moral universe bends toward justice, King argued, is most proximately because "The struggle for freedom on the part of oppressed people in general and the American Negro in particular is not suddenly going to disappear." More fundamentally, it is because "God is on the side of justice." That is why, he continued, "in Montgomery, Alabama, we can walk and never get weary, because we know that there will be a great camp meeting in the promised land of freedom and justice." Martin Luther King Jr., "Out of the Long Night," *The Gospel Messenger* 107, no. 6 (February 8, 1958), page 3 onward, published weekly by the General Brotherhood Board, Elgin, IL, https://tinyurl.com/2p8vpd73. For the origin of the Parker statement, see "The Arc of the Moral Universe Is Long, But It Bends Toward Justice," Quote Investigator, accessed February 14, 2023, https://tinyurl.com/b2jxppz4.

30   Martin Luther King Jr., "Letter from Birmingham Jail," letterfromjail.com, April 16, 1963, https://tinyurl.com/3wdnsf9f.

31   Edward Ball, *Slaves in the Family* (New York: Farrar, Straus & Giroux, 1998).

Chapter 3

1   I found this useful framing in Christopher Grasso's helpful characterization of the so-called Great Awakening: "The Awakening had been dominated by a single question: 'What must I do to be saved?' The Awakening ended as factions formed that proclaimed different answers." Christopher Grasso, *A Speaking Aristocracy: Transforming Public Discourse in Eighteenth-Century Connecticut* (Williamsburg: Omohundro Institute of Early American History & Culture), 96.

2   Alexander Pope's summation is characteristic of this view:

> Vast Chain of Being! which from God began,
> Natures ethereal, human, angel, man,
> Beast, bird, fish, insect, what no eye can see,
> No glass can reach; from Infinite to thee,
> From thee to Nothing.—On superior powers
> Were we to press, inferior might on ours:
> Or in the full creation leave a void,
> Where, one step broken, the great scale's destroyed:
> From Nature's chain whatever link you strike.
> Tenth or ten thousandth, breaks the chain alike. (I.8.233–46)
>
> Alexander Pope, *An Essay on Man; In Epistles to a Friend,*
> *Part I* (London: printed for J. Wilford, 1732), 19.

3   "And therefore as every man is wholly Gods own portion by the title of creation; so all our labours and care, all our powers and faculties must be wholly imployed in the service of God, even all the dayes of our life, that this life being ended, we may live with him forever." Jeremy Taylor, *The rule and exercises of holy living. In which are described the means and instruments of obtaining every vertue, and the remedies against every vice, and considerations serving to the resisting all temptations. Together with prayers containing the whole duty of a Christian, and the parts of devotion fitted to all occasions, and furnish'd for all necessities* (London: printed [by R. Norton] for Richard Royston, 1650), 1, 59.

4   Evidence of their availability in North America is found in their regular listing in catalogues of books for sale.

5   John Bunyan, *The Pilgrim's Progress from this World to that which is to Come* (London: printed for Robert Ponder, 1693).

6   For one discussion of this lasting influence, see Ruth K. MacDonald, *Christian's Children: The Influence of John Bunyan's* The Pilgrim's Progress *on American Children's Literature* (New York: Peter Lang, 1989). Because the trials and tribulations of the young Pilgrim became touchstones for children's literature produced in the era of the early American Republic, McDonald sees its greatest influence in North America in the decades leading up to the US Civil War.

7   Richard Hakluyt, *The Principal Navigations, Voyages, Traffiques and Discoveries of the English Nation* (London: 1589).

8   Peter Mancall, *Hakluyt's Promise: An Elizabethan's Obsession for English America* (New Haven, CT: Yale University Press, 2007), 161, 177, 193.

9   J. H. Elliott, *The Old World and the New, 1492–1650,* Canto ed. (New York: Cambridge University Press, 1970).

10 The first quote is cited in Mancall, *Hakluyt's Promise*, 193. The second is cited in Edmund S. Morgan, *American Slavery, American Freedom: The Ordeal of Colonial Virginia* (New York: Norton, 1995, 1975), 16–17.

11 For further discussion, see Morgan, *American Slavery, American Freedom*, 116.

12 Vincent Carretta, *Equiano the African: Biography of a Self-Made Man* (Athens: University of Georgia Press, 2005), 20.

13 J. K. Thornton, *Africa and Africans in the Making of the Atlantic World, 1400–1800*, 2nd ed. (New York: Cambridge University Press, 1998), 74. In Thornton's assessment, up to this point, the slave trade had grown out of economic relations which were indigenous to Africa and were "in many ways the functional equivalent of the landlord–tenant relationship in Europe." The early slave trade "was rationalized by the African societies who participated in it and had complete control over it until the slaves were loaded onto European ships for transfer to Atlantic societies." Since land could not be purchased in Africa, he explains, wealth could be accumulated principally through the acquisition of slaves as "heritable, wealth-producing dependents." And "Just as slavery took the place of landed property in Africa, so slave raids were the equivalent to wars of conquest," 55, 97, 125.

14 This analysis is from Morgan, *American Slavery, American Freedom*, 90ff. The massacre of 1622 "released all restraints that the company had hitherto imposed on those who thirsted for the destruction and enslavement of the Indians. . . . Within two or three years of the massacre the English had avenged the deaths of that day many times over," 99–100.

15 Most of these laborers were unmarried men who came on contracts under which they were promised freedom and a plot of land upon completion of their term (often seven years). In practice, however, few ever attained these rewards. Many (perhaps most) did not survive the period of their indenture, and many of those who did survive fell quickly into debt as freedmen, which in turn led them directly back to servitude. In short, Morgan summarized, Virginia's plantation-holding elite grew rich by reducing other Virginians to a condition just short of slavery, through a "tightening of labor discipline" that was the first move "toward a system of labor that treated men as things." Morgan, *American Slavery, American Freedom*, 123, 211, 221, 225. "Servitude in Virginia's tobacco fields approached closer to slavery than anything known at the time in England. Men served longer, were subjected to more rigorous punishments, were traded about as commodities already in the 1620s," 297.

16 R. S. Dunn, *Sugar and Slaves: The Rise of the Planter Class in the English West Indies, 1624–1713* (Chapel Hill: University of North Carolina Press, 2000).

17 Enslaving Indians had never proven successful, and Virginians had long ago embraced the notion that the path of least resistance was simply expelling Native peoples from their lands. Besides, importing African slaves did not require Virginians to enslave anyone—a practice widely viewed as morally questionable when undertaken outside of formal warfare. Instead, they could simply buy people who were already enslaved, after the mercenary and moral risks had been taken on by others. For more on the morality of the slave trade in context, see Thornton, *Africa and Africans in the Making of the Atlantic World.*

18 Gordon-Reed, *The Hemingses of Monticello,* 45.

19 According to Morgan, "the actions that produced slavery in Virginia, the individual purchase of slaves instead of servants, and the public protection of masters in their coercion of unwilling labor, had no necessary connection with race. . . . the daily life of a slave differed from that of a servant less drastically than at first sight it appears to have . . . and masters, initially at least, perceived slaves in much the same way they had always perceived servants." "[t]he use of slaves . . . must be viewed in the context of contemporary English attitudes toward the poor and schemes for putting them to work." Morgan, *American Slavery, American Freedom,* 320.

20 "European chattel slavery antedated the development of racist thinking; it was not until the nineteenth century that racism became a well-defined ideology distinguishable from ethnocentrism. . . . Racism was congruent with the new Darwinian current of thought in the biological sciences." van den Berghe, *Race and Racism,* 17.

21 In Morgan's summation, "They were both, after all, basically uncivil, unchristian, and, above all, unwhite." Morgan, *American Slavery, American Freedom,* 329.

22 Thornton, *Africa and Africans,* 116–17. According to Thornton, this growth was not even across regions, but concentrated in Angola and the Lower Guinea region.

23 As Woody Holton has noted, "Fewer than 5 percent of New England and middle colonies residents were enslaved. But given that two-thirds of North American grain, forest products, and livestock ended up on Caribbean sugar plantations, the colonies between New Hampshire and Pennsylvania were as dependent on the work of African Americans as Virginia and South Carolina. In the vitally important economic sphere they, too, were slave societies." Holton, *Liberty Is Sweet,* 28.

24 Holton, *Liberty Is Sweet*, 20–23.

25 The first data point is from Shy, *A People Numerous and Armed*, 123. The second is from Bernard Bailyn, *Voyagers to the West* (New York: Knopf, 1986), 25.

26 While lacking the freedom to consent as we understand it today, some enslaved women—and Gordon-Reed allows that Sally Hemings may have been one—"were amenable to unions with white men who were their legal masters—relationships that worked very much to their advantage and to the advantages of their children and later descendants." Gordon-Reed, *The Hemingses of Monticello*, 106, 115, 353.

27 Morgan, *American Slavery, American Freedom*, 313, 331.

28 Shy summed up the dynamic this way: "Blacks, who had done so much to solve the chronic labor shortage, caused a growing fear of bloody insurrection, especially after about 1740, when New York City and South Carolina had each felt the terror of slave uprisings." Shy, *A People Numerous and Armed*, 123.

29 Quoted in Albert J. Raboteau, *Slave Religion: The "Invisible Institution" in the Antebellum South* (New York: Oxford University Press, 1978), 130.

30 Samuel Davies, *The Duty of Christians to Propagate their Religion among Heathens: Earnestly Recommended to the Masters of Negroe Slaves in Virginia. A Sermon preached in Hanover January 8, 1757* (London: printed by J. Oliver in Bartholomew-Close, 1758).

31 As chronicled by R. Isabela Morales, "Samuel Davies owned at least two slaves while living in Virginia during the 1750s, justifying the practice by framing himself as a benevolent master. In one sermon he delivered in 1755, Davies directly addressed the enslaved people he saw attending the worship service, stating: "You know I have shewn a tender concern for your welfare, ever since I have been in the colony: and you may ask my own negroes whether I treat them kindly or no." See R. Isabela Morales, "Samuel Davies," Princeton & Slavery, accessed February 9, 2023, https://tinyurl.com/4869r52k. The quote is from Samuel Davies, "On the Defeat of General Braddock, Going to Forte-De-Quesne," in *Sermons on Important Subjects, by the Late Reverend and Pious Samuel Davies, A.M. Some Time President of the College in New Jersey* (Boston: Lincoln & Edmands, 1810), 126.

32 See "The Holy Club," Wesley Center Online, accessed February 9, 2023, https://tinyurl.com/ycxw5dya. By contrast to Whitefield's, the Wesleys' experience in Georgia was an abject failure. Charles failed to win over either Indians or settlers at Fort Frederica, where he was appointed chaplain, and John's contentious stay as the pastor of his Savannah parish was scarred by a broken romance, which he

handled badly. Upon their return to England, the Wesleys shared dramatic spiritual experiences, which they came to describe as "conversions." Newly inspired, they went on to launch a grassroots movement of renewal that would dramatically alter England's ecclesial landscape, Charles producing a vast corpus of compelling spiritual hymns, and John creating an ever-expanding network of lay preachers, organized in "circuits."

33 See Ann Taves, *Fits, Trances, & Visions: Experiencing Religion and Explaining Experience from Wesley to James* (Princeton, NJ: Princeton University Press, 1999), 64. See also Jon Butler, *Awash in a Sea of Faith: Christianizing the American People* (Cambridge, MA: Harvard University Press, 1990), 104.

34 Harry S. Stout, *The Divine Dramatist: George Whitefield and the Rise of Modern Evangelicalism* (Grand Rapids, MI: William B. Eerdmans, 1991), 85–95.

35 Anonymous, *The Spirit of the Martyrs Revived in the Doctrines of the Reverend George Whitefield, and the Judicious, and Faithful Methodists* (London: T. Cooper, 1740), 3.

36 "George Whitefield On Slavery," 1751, accessed February 9, 2023, https://tinyurl.com/ewbw5tjd.

37 "The Slave Trade; An Original Letter from Patrick Henry," *New York Times* archive, July 9, 1860, p. 2, https://tinyurl.com/yc7hfw3n.

38 Shy cites a couple of relevant datapoints: "To the relatively homogeneous English population of the seventeenth century were added about 200,000 Scotch-Irish and almost 100,000 Germans in the four decades after 1715." Shy, *A People Numerous and Armed*, 123.

39 Thomas Jefferson, *Notes on the State of Virginia* (Philadelphia: J. T. Rawle, 1801). Jefferson had written notes throughout his lifetime, not intending them for publication, but he began to compile them in 1781 in response to the inquiry of "a foreigner of Distinction, then residing among us." Published in 1787, the notes gave an unfiltered view of Jefferson's true thoughts.

40 Jefferson's fear of a race war—"convulsions which will probably never end but in the extermination of the one or the other race"— was palpable: "Indeed I tremble for my country when reflect that God is just: that his justice cannot sleep for ever: that considering numbers, nature and natural means only, a revolution of the wheel of fortune, an exchange of situation, is among possible events: that it may become probable by supernatural interference! The Almighty has no attribute which can take side with us in such a contest."

41 For a carefully crafted timeline of the relationship, see Gordon-Reed, *The Hemingses of Monticello*, 253ff. Gordon-Reed's majestic book

chronicles the extraordinary lives of Sally and her family, illustrating with elegant nuance the practice of slaveholding in early Virginia. Rather than fetishize the relationship between Thomas Jefferson and Sally Hemings, Gordon-Reed situates it within a web comprising many relationships, each one born from complex negotiations characterized by grossly unequal distribution of power between masters and slaves. In 2018 the Thomas Jefferson Foundation acknowledged publicly what had by then become widely accepted, that Sally Hemings' six children were fathered by Thomas Jefferson. See "Monticello Affirms Thomas Jefferson Fathered Children with Sally Hemings," Monticello.org, accessed February 9, 2023, https://tinyurl.com/2p8pfwz8.

42 As part of their prolific June 1793 correspondence, Thomas Jefferson updated George Washington on his latest thoughts on "calculating what were the profits of a capital invested in Virginia agriculture." Among his observations were his newfound appreciation of the value that sheep added by increasing the productivity of land: "I had never before considered with due attention the profit from that animal." "To George Washington from Thomas Jefferson, 28 June 1793," *Founders Online*, National Archives, accessed February 9, 2023, https://tinyurl.com/3ky5zrmw. Original source: *The Papers of George Washington*, Presidential Series, vol. 13, *1 June–31 August 1793*, ed. Christine Sternberg Patrick (Charlottesville: University of Virginia Press, 2007), 152–54.

43 "Thomas Jefferson to William Thornton, 27 [June] 1810," *Founders Online*, National Archives, accessed February 9, 2023, https://tinyurl.com/y66nspse. Original source: *The Papers of Thomas Jefferson*, Retirement Series, vol. 2, *16 November 1809 to 11 August 1810*, ed. J. Jefferson Looney (Princeton, NJ: Princeton University Press, 2005), 492–93.

44 "Thomas Jefferson to James Madison, 13 May 1810," *Founders Online*, National Archives, accessed February 9, 2023, https://tinyurl.com/26jbsdxz. Original source: *The Papers of Thomas Jefferson*, Retirement Series, vol. 2, *16 November 1809 to 11 August 1810*, 388–90. Jefferson proposed: "if, of our present stock of common ewes, we place with the ram as many as he may be competent to, suppose 50. we may sell the male lambs of every year for such reasonable price as, in addition to the wool, will pay for the maintenance of the flock. the 1st year they will be ½ bloods, the 2^{d} ¾ the 3^{d} ⅞ & the 4th full blooded, if we take care, in selling annually half the ewes also, to keep those of highest blood. this will be a fund for kindnesses to our friends, as well as for indemnification to ourselves; & our whole state may thus, from this small stock, so dispensed, be filled in a very few

years, with this valuable race, & more satisfaction result to ourselves than money ever administered to the bosom of a shaver."

45 The underline of the word "white" is in the original. "Thomas Jefferson to Francis C. Gray, 4 March 1815," *Founders Online*, National Archives, accessed February 9, 2023, https://tinyurl.com/2t2eskkn. Original source: *The Papers of Thomas Jefferson*, Retirement Series, vol. 8, *1 October 1814 to 31 August 1815*, ed. J. Jefferson Looney (Princeton, NJ: Princeton University Press, 2011), 310–12.

46 "From Thomas Jefferson to Henri Grégoire, 25 February 1809," *Founders Online*, National Archives, accessed February 9, 2023, https://tinyurl.com/3catsuvy.

47 "From Thomas Jefferson to Chastellux, 7 June 1785," *Founders Online*, National Archives, accessed February 9, 2023, https://tinyurl.com/mvdy4rmt. Original source: *The Papers of Thomas Jefferson*, vol. 8, *25 February–31 October 1785*, ed. Julian P. Boyd (Princeton, NJ: Princeton University Press, 1953), 184–86.

48 Jefferson continued: "I advance it therefore as a suspicion only, that the blacks, whether originally a distinct race, or made distinct by time and circumstances, are inferior to the whites in the endowments both of body and mind. It is not against experience to suppose, that different species of the same genus, or varieties of the same species, may possess different qualifications. Will not a lover of natural history then, one who views the gradations in all the races of animals with the eye of philosophy, excuse an effort to keep those in the department of man as distinct as nature has formed them?" Jefferson, *Notes on the State of Virginia*, 281.

49 These quotations are drawn from a fine example of this cherry-picking, see Matthew Spalding, "How to Understand Slavery and the American Founding," The Heritage Foundation, August 26, 2002, https://tinyurl.com/2chza4de.

50 The quotes are from Spalding, "How to Understand Slavery and the American Founding." A few months before his death, in July 1826, Thomas Jefferson wrote to a friend on the subject: "The revolution in public opinion which this cause requires, is not to be expected in a day, or perhaps in an age; but time, which outlives all things, will outlive this evil also." To James Heaton, Monticello, May 20, 1826, 1826052.

51 "George Washington's Last Will and Testament, 9 July 1799," Founders Online, accessed February 9, 2023, https://tinyurl.com/55y9brba.

52 According to Gordon-Reed, after accompanying Thomas Jefferson to France and discovering that he could live there as a free man, James Hemings (Sally's brother) negotiated a writ of manumission

from Thomas Jefferson in exchange for his return to Virginia. She also chronicles the bargain by which Hemings returned to Virginia as Jefferson's concubine in exchange for the commitment that her children would be manumitted upon their reaching an age of maturity (Gordon-Reed, *The Hemingses of Monticello*, 326ff.). The pattern by which Sally negotiated the manumission of her family members was well established, although it is not known exactly what negotiations went into the crafting of Jefferson's will.

53 "Last Will and Testament," Thomas Jefferson's Monticello, accessed February 9, 2023, https://tinyurl.com/7npce43e.

54 Morgan, *American Slavery, American Freedom*, 4.

55 Van den Berghe, *Race and Racism*, 78.

56 "Racism thus absorbed in Virginia the fear and contempt that men in England, whether Whig or Tory, monarchist or republican, felt for the inarticulate lower classes." Morgan, *American Slavery, American Freedom*, 385–86. For a good summary of the scholarly consensus on this, see the statement adopted by the adopted by the Executive Board of the American Anthropological Association on May 17, 1998: "AAA Statement on Race," https://tinyurl.com/3ff97nxj.

57 In van den Berghe's estimation: "with the exception of the two Adamses and Garfield, all Presidents openly expressed racial prejudice in and out of office until the 1950s. Some like Jackson and Theodore Roosevelt were even virulent bigots, although most of them simply reflected majority attitudes. The only President to emerge as distinctly antiracist and fully 'modern' in his outlook on race was John Quincy Adams." Van den Berghe, *Race and Racism*, 94–95.

58 Spalding, "How to Understand Slavery and the American Founding."

59 Philip S. Gorski and Samuel L. Perry, "With the Buffalo Massacre, White Christian Nationalism Strikes Again," Washington Post, May 20, 2022, https://tinyurl.com/2duearun.

60 "The Slave Trade; An Original Letter from Patrick Henry," *New York Times* archive, July 9, 1860.

61 Gordon-Reed, *The Hemingses of Monticello*, 119.

62 Quote by John Adams: "Negro Slavery is an evil of Colossal magnitude . . .," Goodreads.com, accessed February 9, 2023, https://tinyurl.com/yh77e2ru.

Chapter 4

1 The clergyman was John Foxe, whose famous martyrology will be discussed in the next chapter; *The Benefit and Invention of Printing by John Fox, that Famous Martyrologist. Extracted out of his Acts and Monuments*, vol. 1 Edit. 9. Anno 1684, 803–4.

2 Richard Baxter, *A call to the unconverted, to turn and live and accept of mercy while mercy may be had, as ever they would find mercy in the day of their extremity. From the living God. To which are added, forms of prayer for morning and evening for a family, for a penitent sinner, and for the Lord's Day. Written at the request of the late Reverend and learned Archbishop Usher. By Richard Baxter. To be read in families where any are unconverted* (Boston: printed for S. Kneeland & T. Green, for D. Henchman in Cornhill, J. Phillips at the Stationers Arms, & T. Hancock at the Bible and Three Crowns in Annstreet, 1731), 11.

3 Baxter, *A call to the unconverted*, D2ff.

4 Frederick B. Tolles, *Quakers and the Atlantic Culture* (New York: Octagon Books, 1960), 11.

5 Hilary Gatti, ed. *Essays on Giordano Bruno* (Princeton, NJ: Princeton University Press, 2011), 155. According to Gatti, "It was in reply to this question that the reformers developed in radical terms the doctrine of Saint Augustine, which had both Platonic and Pauline origins, of an inner light within the mind which guides the believer towards the divine light of truth."

6 Quoted in Tolles, *Quakers and the Atlantic Culture*, 13.

7 David D. Hall, *Cultures of Print: Essays in the History of the Book* (Amherst: University of Massachusetts Press, 1996), 62.

8 By the mid-century, printing presses were up and running at Portsmouth in New Hampshire; Salem, Worcester, and Newbury in Massachusetts; Newport and Providence in Rhode Island; New London, New Haven, Hartford, and Norwich in Connecticut; Albany in New York; Trenton in New Jersey; Annapolis in Maryland; Wilmington in Delaware; Williamsburg in Virginia; and Halifax in North Carolina. For an excellent early summary of this spread of print in the colonies of British North America, see Lawrence C. Wroth's *The Colonial Printer* (New York: Dover, 1994), first published in 1931.

9 See Gary B. Nash, *First City: Philadelphia and the Forging of Historical Memory* (Philadelphia: University of Pennsylvania Press, 2002).

10 Walter Isaacson, *A Benjamin Franklin Reader* (New York: Simon & Schuster, 2005), 445.

11 For instance, the first newspaper ever published in North America, Benjamin Harris's "genuine periodical journal," had been suppressed by the Council of the Massachusetts Bay Colony almost immediately upon its release in September 1690; *Publick Occurrences both Foreign and Domestick*," a small folio of two leaves with a colophon on page three, reading: "Boston, printed by R. Pierce, for Benjamin Harris, at the London-Coffee-House.

1690." Fifteen years later, when Bartholomew Green launched a new weekly, *The Boston Newsletter*, its first issue, dated April 24, 1704, made clear that it was published "by authority" of then Massachusetts Governor Joseph Dudley. *The Boston News-Letter*, April 24, 1704, published by authority and "Printed by B. Green . . . "; Wroth, *The Colonial Printer*, 19. In Virginia, the colony's royal governors took this threat seriously, outlawing printing of any kind up through the year 1690. Even after that date they retained the right to license—and, conversely, forbid—all manner of publication. Quoted in Cynthia Z. and Gregory A. Stiverson, "The Colonial Retail Book Trade: Availability and Affordability of Reading Material in Mid-Eighteenth-Century Virginia," in William Leonard Joyce and American Antiquarian Society, eds., *Printing and Society in Early America* (Worcester: American Antiquarian Society, 1983), 148.

12 Patrick G. Williams, "Franklin, James (1697–1735), printer," *American National Biography*, June 7, 2018. For more on this, see Jessica Choppin Roney, *Governed by a Spirit of Opposition: The Origins of American Political Practice in Colonial Philadelphia* (Baltimore: Johns Hopkins University Press, 2014).

13 See the introductory note to "Silence Dogood, No. 8, 9 July 1722," *Founders Online*, National Archives, accessed February 10, 2023, https://tinyurl.com/4kun8ye2. Original source: *The Papers of Benjamin Franklin*, vol. 1, *January 6, 1706 through December 31, 1734*, ed. Leonard W. Labaree (New Haven, CT: Yale University Press, 1959), 27–30.

14 Franklin joined with Hugh Gaine to buy *The Universal Instructor in all Arts and Sciences: and Pennsylvania Gazette*, which Samuel Keiner had begun printing the previous year. Franklin shortened the title to *The Pennsylvania Gazette*. See the Accessible Archives, accessed February 10, 2023, https://tinyurl.com/2zsapy3c.

15 Entirely representative was an "Attempt towards an EPITAPH" published after the 1737 death of Queen Caroline, the wife of England's King George II. *The Philadelphia Gazette* (Philadelphia, PA), June 1, 1738, 2. Also typical is this poem "On the Death of the late celebrated Mrs. Rowe," a poet named Elizabeth Rowe whose tremendously popular poems on *The Friendship of Death*, constructed in the form of letters written from the dead to the living, earned her fame on both sides of the Atlantic. *The Philadelphia Gazette* (Philadelphia, PA), July 26, 1739, 2.

16 For more on this, see Roney, *Governed by a Spirit of Opposition*.

17 "Apology for Printers, 10 June 1731," *Founders Online*, National Archives, accessed February 10, 2023, https://tinyurl.com/bdcvuyj9.

Original source: *The Papers of Benjamin Franklin*, vol. 1, *January 6, 1706 through December 31, 1734*, 194–99.

18 By the turn of the eighteenth century, students and tutors at Harvard College had been producing almanacs for decades. While neither was schooled at Harvard, James and Benjamin Franklin were raised in this literary environment, and they sought early on in their publishing careers to capitalize on it. From his publishing house on Queen Street in Boston, James first printed Nathan Bowen's *New England Diary and Almanack* in 1725, and then, after opening a press in Newport, Rhode Island, produced under the pseudonym "Poor Robin" his own *The Rhode-Island Almanack*, the first issue printed in 1727 (for the year 1728).

19 See Benjamin Franklin (Richard Saunders pseudonym), *Poor Richard, 1733, An Almanack for the Year of Christ 1733* (Philadelphia: Benjamin Franklin, 1733).

20 T. J. Tomlin cites one instructive data point: "Franklin's business partner, David Hall, reported that between 1752 and 1765 he printed 141,257 copies of *Poor Richard's Almanack* (averaging around 10,000 per year); this alone equaled one almanac per one hundred colonists." Tomlin, "Astrology's from Heaven Not from Hell," *Early American Studies* 8, no. 2 (Spring 2010): 294.

21 Hall, *Cultures of Print*, 91. In summing up this tradition, I also relied on T. J. Tomlin's summation as found in Tomlin, "Astrology's from Heaven Not from Hell," 321.

22 See, for example, Hall, *Cultures of Print*, 4–5.

23 In this Franklin was following a well-traveled path—new publishers in North America routinely opened their houses by selling "steady sellers" like Bibles, psalm books, and primers, while simultaneously printing locally authored works that they hoped would be found attractive by the readers in their local markets. Working closely with printers, booksellers, bookbinders, newspaper editors, and authors—and often working in more than one of these capacities themselves—homegrown American publishers expanded dramatically their share of the growing North American market, even as the bulk of print material consumed in the colonies continued to be imported from London. A representation of what Franklin offered for sale can be found in the summary listing of items "Sold by the Printer hereof," with which he concluded his *Poor Richard's Almanac*, as in this 1733 edition: "Large Quarto Bibles of good print, small Bibles, Testaments, Psalters, Primers, Hornbooks, Account-books, Demi-royal and small Paper, Ink, Ink-powder, Dutch Quills, Wafers, New Version of Psalms, Watts's Psalms, Practice of Piety, Whole Duty of Man, Barclay's Apology, Beavan's Primitive Christianity,

Vade mecum, New Help to Discourse, Pope's Miscellany Poems, Life Actions and End of Dr. Faustus, Aristotle's Works, Argalus and Parthenia, History of Fortunatus, with several other diverting and entertaining Histories."

24 Christopher Phillips, "Cotton Mather Brings Isaac Watt's Hymns to America; or How to Perform a Hymn without Singing It," *The New England Quarterly* 85, no. 2 (2012): 203.

25 Watts himself recognized as much. As he put it in the preface to the edition of *Hymns and Spiritual Songs*: "The whole Book is written in four Sorts of Metre, and fitted to the most Common Tunes. . . . The Metaphors are generally sunk to the Level of vulgar Capacities. . . . Some of the Beauties of Poesy are neglected, and some wilfully defaced . . . lest a more exalted Turn or Though or Language should darken or disturb the Devotion of the weakest Souls. . . . I have avoided the more obscure and controverted Points of Christianity, that we might all obey the Direction of the Word of God, and sing his Praises with Understanding, Psalm xlvii, 7. The Contentions and distinguishing Words of Sects and Parties are secluded, that whole Assemblies might assist at the Harmony, and different Churches join in the same Worship, without Offence." Watts, *Hymns and Spiritual Songs in Three Books . . . The Thirty Third Edition* (London: Longman and Ware, 1771).

26 Isaac Watts, *Hymns and Spiritual Songs* (Boston: ????, 1720?). The only known copy, held by the Massachusetts Historical Society, lacks the title page and is otherwise imperfect. Title, edition statement, and imprint supplied by Bristol. By 1812 the volume had been reprinted in one form or another in America at least eighty-four times, and the work was such standard fare that new printers routinely included their own print runs of the songbook almost immediately upon attempting to break into established markets. Watts's *Divine Songs Attempted in Easy Language for the Use of Children* was printed even more widely, the audience multiplied many times over by its popularity as a "hand-me-down." Phillips, "Cotton Mather Brings Isaac Watt's Hymns to America," 203.

27 William T. Dargan, *Lining Out the Word: Dr. Watts Hymn Singing in the Music of Black Americans: William T. Dargan* (Berkeley: University of California Press, 2006), 94. In Dargan's assessment, "performances of Watts's lyrics became an artistic watershed for language contact between slave dialects and English verse," to such an extent that an entirely unique and distinctively American style of singing was born, which would come to be known across the African American landscape as, simply, "Dr. Watts." By the mid-eighteenth century,

Dargan concludes, Watts "had become renowned in England and abroad, and his paraphrase of Psalm 90, 'Our God, Our Help in Ages Past,' had become a signal moment in the English Puritan epoch."

28 Charles Wesley, William Cowper, and others who left important marks were, by their own estimation, following in Watts's footsteps.

29 See, for instance, Gilbert Tennent's sermon, *The danger of an unconverted ministry, considered in a sermon on Mark VI. 34. Preached at Nottingham, in Pennsylvania, March 8. anno 1739,40. By Gilbert Tennent, A.M. and Minister of the Gospel in New-Brunswick, New-Jersey. [Five lines from Jeremiah]* (Philadelphia: printed by Benjamin Franklin, in Market-Street, 1740). Or, as Samuel Davies put it in *Religion and Public Spirit*, a sermon published by Daniel Fowle in 1762: "The New Birth is the Beginning of All Genuine Religion and Virtue: it is your first Entrance into the World of Usefulness; and an Incorporation with the Society of Saints and Angels, and all the beneficent Beings in the Universe." Samuel Davies, *Religion and Public Spirit* (Portsmouth, NH: Daniel Fowle, 1762), 13.

30 As Rath has documented, these practices combined with practices of Native peoples and African slaves and their descendants— drumming, shouting, stomping, groaning, war-crying, for instance—to create an entirely new American "soundscape." Richard Cullen Rath, *How Early America Sounded* (Ithaca, NY: Cornell University Press, 2003). This new sonic environment was one of profound mutual influence, even as the English were, characteristically, unaware of how their own behaviors were being changed, and even as they routinely portrayed their own soundings as "civilized," while deeming those of others as "savage" or "backward." See David Cressy, *Bonfires and Bells: National Memory and the Protestant Calendar in Elizabethan and Stuart England* (Berkeley: University of California Press, 1989), 50ff.

31 For generations this fact inspired puzzlement—or avoidance— among Franklin's biographers, who preferred to cast his life journey as a one-dimensional and unilinear unfolding of reasoned speculation. More recently, historians like Peter Charles Hoffer have described what they see as an "unexpected partnership" as born from a shared conviction that the "Atlantic world could be knit together more closely with words." Peter Charles Hoffer, *When Benjamin Franklin Met the Reverend Whitefield: Enlightenment, Revival, and the Power of the Printed Word* (Baltimore: John Hopkins University Press, 2013), 5. But the words in which people as disparate in their views as Franklin and Whitefield found such resonance were not devoid of content. To the contrary, they were words that comprised a common Protestant vernacular that

writers and publishers, preachers, and hymnodists, used to construct bridges of common sentiment across cultural gaps in the
colonial landscape. Philadelphia became the principal platform
from which this vernacular was propagated across the middle
decades of the eighteenth century.

32 *The Philadelphia Gazette* (Philadelphia, PA), December 27, 1739.
His biographer Harry S. Stout has called Whitefield's style "biblical
history in a theatrical key." Stout, *The Divine Dramatist*, 104. In his
year-end edition of *The Pennsylvania Gazette*, Franklin reprinted
this poem "To the Rev. Mr. Whitefield" from the *London Gazette*:

> SWEET is thy voice, and manly is thy strain,
> Nor does thy wak'ng trumpet sound in vain.
> Then still go on, proclaim thy Master's laws.
> Warm'd with the promise of thy Lord's applause,
> In that important, that tremendous day,
> When seas shall vanish, rocks shall melt away;
> When the great Judge impartially shall trace
> The various actions of the human race.
>
> > "On Hearing George Whitefield at the New Building in
> > Philadelphia," *The Philadelphia Gazette* (Philadelphia, PA),
> > December 18, 1740.

33 Jonathan Lyons, *The Society for Useful Knowledge: How Benjamin
Franklin and Friends Brought the Enlightenment to America* (New
York: Bloomsbury Press, 2013).

34 See Peter R. Silver, *Our Savage Neighbors: How Indian War Transformed
Early America* (New York: W. W. Norton, 2008), 301. According
to Silver, this rhetoric and identity would prove indispensable to the
colonists as they fought wars not just against the Delaware and other
Native peoples—the Conestogas, Tuscaroras, Tutelos, Naticokes,
Conestogas, Shawnees, and Senecas—but also, ironically, against
the French and, finally, the British. The "crises of Indian war," Silver
concludes, "had tilted public life toward the celebration of a suffering people, creating a new politics that was harsh and ruthless, if
recognizably democratic."

35 *Observations concerning the Increase of Mankind, Peopling of Countries,&c.* (Boston: printed and sold by S. Kneeland in Queen-Street,
1755).

36 David Copeland in Carol Sue Humphrey, *The American Revolution
and the Press: The Promise of Independence* (Evanston, IL: Medill
School of Journalism/Northwestern University Press, 2013), xi.

37 As his biographer Jane Calvert has noted, only at the end of the
nineteenth century did historians dub Dickinson "the Penman of

the Revolution," but the rationale for the nickname is easy to understand. Dickinson first earned a colony-wide reputation in 1765 as the "de facto leader of the Stamp Act Congress, and the draftsman of the Resolutions of the Congress." His true renown came when his identity was revealed as the author of *Letters from a Farmer in Pennsylvania*. As a delegate to the Continental Congress, Dickinson was "the author of, in addition to many other . . . documents, the First Petition to the King (1774), *An Address from Congress to the Inhabitants of Quebec* (1774), the Olive Branch Petition (1775), the Declaration for Taking Up Arms (1775) and the first draft of the Articles of Confederation (1776)." Jane E. Calvert, *Quaker Constitutionalism and the Political Thought of John Dickinson* (New York: Cambridge University Press, 2009), 38.

38 Calvert, *Quaker Constitutionalism*, 67.
39 See Arthur M. Schlesinger, "A Note on Songs as Patriot Propaganda 1765–1776," *The William and Mary Quarterly* 11, no. 1 (1954): 78–88.
40 *Connecticut Journal and New-Haven Post Boy* (Boston, MA), August 12, 1768, 2, America's Historical Newspapers, accessed February 24, 2017; *Virginia Gazette* (Charlestown, VA) *December 8, 1768*, 1, America's Historical Newspapers, accessed February 24, 2017. For an example of the broadside advertised, see "Advertisement," *Boston Chronicle* (Boston, MA) from Monday, December 12, to Monday, December 19, 1768, America's Historical Newspapers, accessed February 24, 2017.
41 Christopher Boyd Brown, *Singing the Gospel: Lutheran Hymns and the Success of the Reformation* (Cambridge, MA: Harvard University Press, 2005); Laura Mason, *Singing the French Revolution: Popular Culture and Politics, 1787–1799* (Ithaca, NY: Cornell University Press, 1996).
42 Zac Gershberg and Sean Illing, *The Paradox of Democracy: Free Speech, Open Media, and Perilous Persuasion* (Chicago: University of Chicago Press, 2022).
43 "By the end of the French and Indian War in 1763, there was at least one printing establishment in each of the thirteen mainland colonies and the number of newspapers had grown from eleven in 1736 to twenty-three in 1763." The volume per printer per week grew from five hundred per week in 1750 to "as many as 1500 copies per week" by 1765. Newspapers were sold through subscription, but local taverns or coffeehouses often subscribed and customers either read them directly or listened while someone else read them aloud." Humphrey, *The American Revolution and the Press*, 33.
44 Sir William Berkeley, the longest-tenured of Virginia's seventeenth-century governors, had summarized this suspicion

succinctly: "I thank God, there are no free schools nor printing, and I hope we shall not have these hundred years; for learning has brought disobedience, and heresy, and sects into the world, and printing has divulged them, and libels against the best government. God keep us from both." Quoted in Cynthia Z. and Gregory A. Stiverson, "The Colonial Retail Book Trade," 148.

45 Sidney Kobre, "The Revolutionary Colonial Press—A Social Interpretation," *Journalism Quarterly 20* (1943), quoted in Wroth, *The Colonial Printer*, 20.

46 "From Benjamin Franklin to Cadwalader Evans, 5 [August] 1767," *Founders Online*, National Archives, accessed February 10, 2023, https://tinyurl.com/4tu94amb. Original source: *The Papers of Benjamin Franklin*, vol. 14, *January 1 through December 31, 1767*, 222–24.

Chapter 5

1 John Winthrop, "Model of Christian Charity," accessed February 10, 2023, https://tinyurl.com/ycx5t2sz.

2 The observer, unnamed, was quoted by John Foxe, in his *Actes and Monuments*, which will be treated extensively in the next chapter.

3 "Apology for Printers, 10 June 1731," *Founders Online*, National Archives, accessed February 10, 2023, https://tinyurl.com/bdcvuyj9. Original source: *The Papers of Benjamin Franklin*, vol. 1, *January 6, 1706 through December 31, 1734*, 194–99.

4 As the historian P. R. Silver has summarized, war with the Indians led the colonists to see themselves as "a suffering people" and embraced "a new politics that was harsh and ruthless, if recognizably democratic." Silver, *Our Savage Neighbors*, 301.

5 Conversation with Peter Mancall, University of Southern California, spring 2016.

6 Benjamin Church, *The Times: A Poem* (Boston: Thomas Fleet, 1765).

7 For a good and recent summary of all this, see Holton, *Liberty Is Sweet*, 14–15, 25–26.

8 Eric Hinderaker, *Boston's Massacre* (Cambridge, MA: Harvard University Press, 2017), 47, 61. "Three newspapers—the *Boston Evening-Post*, edited by Thomas Fleet Jr. and John Fleet; the *Boston-Gazette and Evening Journal*, under the joint editorship of John Gill and Benjamin Edes; and John Green and Joseph Russel's *Massachusetts Gazette and Boston Weekly News-Letter*—served as mouthpieces for the movement."

9 Adams's biographer John C. Miller concludes, "The *Independent Advertiser* contains the germ of the ideas for which Adams was to fight for the greater part of his life, ideas which were later to form the

political testament of the Whig Party in the American Revolution."
John C. Miller, *John Adams: Pioneer in Propaganda* (Boston: Little,
Brown & Company, 1936), 11ff.

10 "Instructions of the town of Boston to its representatives in the General Court," May 1764; Harry Alonzo Cushing, ed., *The Writings of Samuel Adams*: vol. 1, *1764–1769* (New York: G. P. Putnam's Sons, 1904), 5.

11 Samuel Adams, John Ruddock, and John Hancock "To the inhabitants of the town of Plymouth," March 24, 1766; Cushing, *The Writings of Samuel Adams*: vol. 1, 72.

12 "Article submitted to Edes & Gill, editors, Boston Gazette," October 17, 1768; Cushing, *The Writings of Samuel Adams*: vol. 1, 251.

13 "Article signed Vindex to Boston Gazette," December 5, 1768; Cushing, *The Writings of Samuel Adams*: vol. 1, 258.

14 "Article signed Vindex to Boston Gazette," December 12, 1768; Cushing, *The Writings of Samuel Adams*: vol. 1, 266.

15 David Copeland in Humphrey, *The American Revolution and the Press*, xii.

16 Adams, 362/363. "Article signed Alfred to Boston Gazette," October 2, 1769.

17 Bailyn, *The Ideological Origins of the American Revolution*, ix.

18 Thomas Paine, *Common Sense; Addressed to the Inhabitants of America On the following interesting Subjects . . . The Third Edition* (Philadelphia: R. Bell, 1776), 13–14.

19 As late as 1774, Benjamin Franklin could write that in America "there is not a single native of our country who is not firmly attached to his King by principle and by affection. But a new kind of loyalty seems to be required of us, a loyalty to Parliament; a loyalty that is to extend, it seems, to a surrender of all our properties, whenever a House of Commons, in which there is not a single member of our choosing, shall think fit to grant them away without our consent." Benjamin Franklin, *The Causes of the Present Distractions in America* (New York: F.B., 1774), 15.

20 Woody Holton sums up the consensus view: "the truth was that no monarch had ruled Great Britain since the 'Glorious Revolution' of 1688. The policies promulgated in the king's name were actually the work of his cabinet: the fewer than ten men who held the highest posts in government. Granted, George had the power of appointment, but he had to choose cabinet secretaries who could command parliamentary majorities. So long as they did so, they could cling to power even in the face of royal disapproval. George III more closely resembled Elizabeth II (1926–)—a figurehead—than the all-but-omnipotent Elizabeth I (1533–1603). Already in 1763, every speech

he gave to Parliament was a ventriloquist act, dictated to him by his ministers." Holton, *Liberty Is Sweet*, 25.

21 "Benjamin Franklin's Great Seal Design," GreatSeal.com. Thomas Jefferson altered Franklin's proposal slightly to describe the version that was recommended by the congressional committee for the reverse side of the seal: "Pharaoh sitting in an open Chariot, a Crown on his head and a Sword in his hand, passing through the divided Waters of the Red Sea in Pursuit of the Israelites: Rays from a Pillar of Fire in the Cloud, expressive of the divine Presence and Command, beaming on Moses who stands on the shore and extending his hand over the Sea causes it to overwhelm Pharaoh."

22 From Mark Noll interview with Liz Covart, *Ben Franklin's World* podcast, episode 073, "Mark Noll, The Bible in Early America," March 15, 2016, https://tinyurl.com/3b7dhwwv.

23 Jill Lepore, "What the January 6th Report Is Missing," *The New Yorker*, January 16, 2023, https://tinyurl.com/mr3ukr3t.

Chapter 6

1 For more on this, see my extended treatment of Henry Grove, *A Discourse Concerning the Nature of the Lord's Supper* (Boston, 1766) in my dissertation: John Fanestil, "The Print Practice of Martyrology in British North America, 1688–1787" (PhD diss., University of Southern California, 2017).

2 Elizabeth Castelli describes these ideas as "hardwired into the collective consciousness of Western culture" and "one of the central legacies of the Christian tradition." Elizabeth A. Castelli, *Martyrdom and Memory: Early Christian Culture Making* (New York: Columbia University Press, 2004), 33. By remaining faithful in final confrontations with ruthless tyrants, the early Christian martyrs earned both the penalty of death and the prize of eternal salvation. During the first centuries of the Christian era, the Greek and Latin words for "witness" came to be linked inextricably to the ideal of the truly virtuous who proved willing to die as "witnesses to the truth." Herbert Musurillo, *The Acts of the Christian Martyrs* (Oxford: Clarendon Press, 1972).

3 In his pioneering early twentieth-century work, the French scholar Hippolyte Delehaye (1859–1941) listed as exemplary of this tradition the accounts of the noble deaths of "Socrates, Anaxarque, Paetus Thrasea, Helvidius Priscus, Rubellius Plautas and Seneca." When the Emperor Vespasian threatened him with death, for instance, Helvidius Priscus is said to have responded: "When did I tell you I was immortal? You play your role and I will play mine. Your role

is to cause my death, mine is to die without trembling." Hippolyte Delehaye, *Les passions des martyrs et les genres littéraires*, 2nd ed. (Brussels: Société des Bollandistes, 1966), 114ff.

4 Performances of martyrdom are inherently public in nature—to be recognized as such, every martyr also requires an audience of people who live to tell the tale. As Daniel Boyarin has written, "even more than tragedy," acts of martyrdom are "deaths that are seen . . . [as] a practice that takes place within the public and, therefore, shared space." Daniel Boyarin, *Dying for God: Martyrdom and the Making of Christianity and Judaism* (Palo Alto: Stanford University Press, 1999), 21.

5 As described in the New Testament letter to the Hebrews: "Wherefore seeing we also are compassed about with so great a cloud of witnesses, let us lay aside every weight, and the sin which doth so easily beset us, and let us run with patience the race that is set before us, Looking unto Jesus the author and finisher of our faith; who for the joy that was set before him endured the cross, despising the shame, and is set down at the right hand of the throne of God" (Hebrews 12:1–2, KJV).

6 Candida Moss observes: "This association of courage, virtue, death, and masculinity meant that the notion of dying well was itself gendered. To die a good death, in or out of battle, entailed dying with self-control. In other words, it meant taking it like a man." Candida Moss, *Ancient Christian Martyrdom: Diverse Practices, Theologies, and Traditions* (New Haven, CT: Yale University Press, 2012), 28–29.

7 John Foxe, *Actes and Monuments* (London: John Day, 1563). Dominic Janes and Alex Houen put the number of burnings under Mary at 284. Janes and Houen, *Martyrdom and Terrorism: Pre-Modern to Contemporary Perspectives* (New York: Oxford University Press, 2014), 63.

8 John Foxe, *The Unabridged Acts and Monuments Online* or *TAMO* (1570 ed.) (Sheffield: HRI Online Publications, 2011), 4, accessed February 14, 2023, https://www.dhi.ac.uk/foxe/.

9 Foxe, *The Unabridged Acts and Monuments Online*, 228.

10 John N. King, *Foxe's* Book of Martyrs *and Early Modern Print Culture* (Cambridge and New York: Cambridge University Press, 2006), xi. For just one example of the scriptural references conjured by this story, see Isaiah 42:2–12. What came to be known simply as Foxe's "Book of Martyrs" remained among the most widely printed books in the English language for over two centuries, as generations of printers abridged, appended, altered, and expanded upon the original. Generations of English Protestants on both sides of the Atlantic

were steeped in Foxe's sharply dualistic and deeply oppositional way of thinking about the Christian faith and were trained to venerate martyrs like Wycliffe and Tyndale—and the hundreds more who were hung from the gallows or burned at the stake—as exemplars of the faith.

11 Foxe, *The Unabridged Acts and Monuments Online*, 1794. The exhortation echoed the heavenly encouragement given to Polycarp, one of the martyrs Foxe heralded in his "first Book containing the first persecutions of the Primitive Church": "And when there was such uproar in the place of execution, that he could not be heard but of a very few, there came a voice from heaven to Polycarpus as he was going into the appointed place of judgment, saying: be of good cheer Polycarpus and play the man." Foxe, 65.

12 Similar phrasing in the King James Version of the Bible is found in the deuterocanonical book of 1 Maccabees, where the elder Mattathias exhorts young Jewish rebels with these words: "Wherefore you my sonnes be valiant, and shew your selues men in the behalfe of the law, for by it shall you obtaine glory . . . " (1 Maccabees 2:64, KJV).

13 Jeremy Taylor, *The great exemplar of sanctity and holy life according to the Christian institution described in the history of the life and death of the ever blessed Jesus Christ the saviour of the world: with considerations and discourses upon the several parts of the story and prayers fitted to the several mysteries: in three parts* (London: printed by R.N. for Francis Ash, 1649); Jeremy Taylor, *Antiquitates christianae, or, The history of the life and death of the holy Jesus as also the lives acts and martyrdoms of his Apostles: in two parts* (London: printed by R. Norton for R. Royston, 1765).

14 Taylor, *The rule and exercises of holy living*, 87.

15 Adrian Chastain Weimer, *Martyrs' Mirror: Persecution and Holiness in Early New England* (Oxford and New York: Oxford University Press, 2011), 49.

16 See my *Mrs. Hunter's Happy Death: Lessons on Living from People Preparing to Die* (New York: Doubleday, 2006).

17 Watts, *Hymns and Spiritual Songs in Three Books . . . The Thirty Third Edition*.

18 The scholar of martyrdom Elizabeth Castelli describes this as the "construction of collective memory," arguing that this way of thinking allows us "to move past often unresolvable questions of 'what really happened'" to ask instead how "communities constitute and sustain themselves" across long expanses of time. Castelli, *Martyrdom and Memory*, 5, 29, 39.

19 Paul Leicester Ford, *The New England Primer: A History of Its Origin and Development* (New York: Dodd, Mead & Co., 1897), cited

in "A Famous Book—The 'New England Primer,'" *New York Times*, November 14, 1897.

20 Anonymous, *The New-England primer improved. For the more easy attaining the true reading of English. To which is added, the Assembly of Divines catechism* (Boston: 1750), 20. In Foxe's rendering, when he was confronted by one of the sheriffs, demanding that he recant his "abominable doctrine," Rogers replied: "That which I have preached I will seal with my blood." When he was set ablaze, Foxe reported, Rogers washed his hands in the flames of the fire as they consumed him.

21 Jerome Griswold has estimated the total number of prints at six million between 1680 and 1830. See Kathleen Connery Fitzgibbons, "A History of the Evolution of the Didactic Literature for Puritan Children in America, 1656–1856" (EdD, University of Massachusetts, 1987).

22 Conversation with Colin Callaway, fall 2018.

23 Jason Farago, "The Myth of North America, in One Painting," *New York Times*, November 25, 2020, https://tinyurl.com/3fduz2f4.

24 Davies, *Religion and Public Spirit*, 4.

25 Within the year, Davies's "curse of cowardice" sermon was reprinted in Boston, New York, and Woodbridge, New Jersey: Samuel Davies, *The curse of cowardice. A sermon preached to the militia of Hanover County, in Virginia, at a general muster, May 8, 1758. With a view to raise a company for Captain Samuel Meredith. By Samuel Davies, A.M.* (London: printed. Boston: re-printed and sold by Z. Fowle and S. Draper, opposite the Lion & Bell, in Marlborough-Street, 1759; Woodbridge, NJ: re-printed and sold by James Parker, 1759; New-York: re-printed and sold by Samuel Parker, at the New-Printing Office in Beaver-Street, 1759).

26 As Mark Noll has observed, the "public biblical religion in the Revolutionary era descended directly from public religion during the French and Indian War." Mark A. Noll, *In the Beginning Was the Word: The Bible in American Public Life, 1492–1783* (Oxford: Oxford University Press, 2016), 292.

27 John Hancock, *An oration; delivered March 5, 1774, at the request of the inhabitants of the town of Boston: to commemorate the bloody tragedy of the fifth of March 1770. By the Honorable John Hancock, Esq; [Five lines in Latin from Virgil]* (Boston: printed by Eddes and Gill, in Queen Street, 1774; Newport, Rhode Island: reprinted and sold by S. Southwick, in Queen-Street, 1774; New-Haven: re-printed by Thomas and Samuel Green, 1774; Philadelphia: printed by J. Douglass M'Dougall, in Chestnut-Street, 1775).

28 Joseph Warren, *An Oration Delivered March the 6th, 1775* (New York: Printed by John Anderson at Beekman's Slip), 15.

29 Ethan S. Rafuse, "Warren, Joseph (1741–1775), physician and patriot leader," in *American National Biography*, 8 June 2018, https://tinyurl.com/4skbcpdc.

30 Quoted in Humphrey, *The American Revolution and the Press*, 113.

31 Hancock, *An oration*.

32 Samuel Stillman, *Death, the last enemy, destroyed by Christ* (Philadelphia: Joseph Crukshank, 1776), iv, 14–15.

33 Abiel Leonard, *A prayer, composed for the benefit of the soldiery, in the American army, to assist them in their private devotions; and recommended to their particular use. By Abiel Leonard, A.M. Chaplain to General Putnam's regiment, in said army* (Cambridge, MA: printed and sold by S. & E. Hall, 1775).

34 Cited in James P. Byrd, *Sacred Scripture, Sacred War: The Bible and the American Revolution* (New York: Oxford University Press, 2013), 12. In the historian Spencer McBride's assessment, these chaplains encouraged soldiers to conceive of themselves "as Christian soldiers, part of a carefully constructed modern Army of Israel dispatched to protect America's providential destiny." Spencer McBride, *Pulpit & Nation: Clergymen and the Politics of Revolutionary America* (Charlottesville: University of Virginia Press, 2016), 12, 35, 41.

35 To name a few: Thomas Symmes's *Lovewell Lamented*, Peter Clark's *Christian Bravery*, William McClenachan's *The Christian Warrior*, Thomas Prentice's *When the People, and the rulers among them, willingly offer themselves to a military expedition against their unrighteous enemies*, William Hobby's *The Soldier Caution'd*, Jonathan Todd's *The Soldier Waxing Strong and Valiant in fight through faith*, Samuel Checkley's *A Day of Darkness*, Isaac Morrill's *The Soldier Exhorted*, Gilbert Tennent's *The Happiness of Rewarding the Enemies of our Religion and Liberty*, and Samuel Davies's *The curse of cowardice*. And to get a sense of the potential for these sermons to make their way through the network of print publication on both sides of the Atlantic, consider Davies, *The curse of cowardice*.

36 See, for example, Robert Eastburn, *A faithful narrative, of the many dangers and sufferings, as well as wonderful and surprizing deliverances of Robert Eastburn, during his late captivity among the Indians: together with some remarks upon the country of Canada, and the religion and policy of its inhabitants; the whole intermixed with devout reflections. By Robert Eastburn. Published at the earnest request of many persons, for the benefit of the public. With a recommendatory preface, by the Rev. Gilbert Tennent. [Six lines from Psalms]* (Philadelphia: printed by William Dunlap, 1758; Boston: re-printed and sold by Green & Russell, opposite the probate-office in Queen-Street, 1758).

37　The details are drawn from the educational displays at the Nathan
　　Hale Schoolhouse, New London, Connecticut, June 19, 2017.
　　"Nathan Hale enlisted in the 7th Connecticut Regiment on Thurs-
　　day, July 6, 1775, and six months later, on January 1, 1776, received
　　his commission, signed by the president of the Congress, John Han-
　　cock, as a regular captain in the Continental Army." See also George
　　Dudley Seymour, *Documentary Life of Nathan Hale: Comprising all
　　Available Official and Private Documents Bearing on the Life of the
　　Patriot, Together with an Appendix, Showing the Background of His
　　Life* . . . (New-Haven: priv. printed for the author, 1941). See also Paul
　　R. Misencik, *The Original American Spies: Seven Covert Agents of the
　　Revolutionary War* (Jefferson, NC: McFarland, 2014), 11–12.

38　Joseph Addison, *Cato. A tragedy, by Mr. Addison. [Seven lines from
　　Seneca]* (Boston: printed by Mein and Fleeming, and sold by J. Mein
　　at the London Book Store, north side of King-Street, 1767), 60.

39　As William Bradford Jr. wrote to his sister Rachel in May 1778 from
　　Washington's encampment at Valley Forge: "[T]he camp could now
　　afford you some entertainment. The manoeuvering of the Army
　　itself is a sight that would charm you.—Besides these, the Theatre is
　　opened—Last Monday Cato was performed before a very numerous
　　and splendid audience. . . . The scenery was in Taste—& the per-
　　formance admirable—Col. George did his part to admiration—he
　　made an excellent die (as they say)." Jason Shaffer, "Making 'an
　　Excellent Die': Death, Mourning, and Patriotism in the Propaganda
　　Plays of the American Revolution," *Early American Literature* 41, no.
　　1 (2006): 1–27.

40　"General Orders, 2 July 1776," *Founders Online*, National Archives,
　　accessed February 14, 2023, https://tinyurl.com/mr43pmt8. Original
　　source: *The Papers of George Washington*, Revolutionary War Series,
　　vol. 5, *16 June 1776–12 August 1776*, ed. Philander D. Chase (Char-
　　lottesville: University Press of Virginia, 1993), 179–82. The entire
　　quote: "Our cruel and unrelenting Enemy leaves us no choice but
　　a brave resistance, or the most abject submission; this is all we can
　　expect—We have therefore to resolve to conquer or die: Our own
　　Country's Honor, all call upon us for a vigorous and manly exer-
　　tion, and if we now shamefully fail, we shall become infamous to the
　　whole world. Let us therefore rely upon the goodness of the Cause,
　　and the aid of the supreme Being, in whose hands Victory is, to ani-
　　mate and encourage us to great and noble Actions."

41　George McKenna has more neatly described this potent admixture
　　as comprising centuries-old "Anti-Catholicism," pan-Protestant
　　celebrations of religious "liberty," and new conceptions of "repub-
　　lican freedom." This admixture lit a fire in the period of the French

and Indian War that in the war's aftermath, McKenna observes, would fuel "an apocalyptic rage against British policies." McKenna, *The Puritan Origins of American Patriotism*, 69.

42 As Alan Fueur of the *New York Times* concluded after following hundreds of prosecutions of people who stormed the US Capitol on January 6, 2021: "People from all 50 states have been prosecuted. Most are white men from middle- or working-class backgrounds, but there are also women, Hispanic people, Black people.... If someone is being criminally prosecuted, there's often some dysfunction in their past. I've been struck by how trauma rests at the center of so many of the Jan. 6 defendants' lives, whether it's poverty, addiction, or deep family dysfunction"; "Hundreds of Jan. 6 Cases," *New York Times*, August 21, 2022, https://tinyurl.com/rkty6szz.

43 "Christian Nationalism and the January 6 Insurrection," accessed February 14, 2023, https://tinyurl.com/4aer3y7m. For a good profile of Greg Locke, see Tim Alberta, "How Politics Poisoned the Evangelical Church," *The Atlantic*, June 2022, https://tinyurl.com/54f8acn3.

44 In November 2022, Ashli Babbitt's brother was convicted of a hate crime for hurling racial slurs while assaulting a San Diego Gas & Electric worker; "Ashli Babbitt's Brother Convicted of Hate Crime against SDG&E Worker," 10 News San Diego, November 9, 2022, https://tinyurl.com/28e39erb. On January 6, 2023, Babbitt's mother was arrested while protesting at the US Capitol for after refusing to comply with police orders; Alia Shoaib, "Ashli Babbitt's Mother Was Arrested on the Second Anniversary of the Capitol Riot in Washington, DC," MSN.com, January 7, 2023, https://tinyurl.com/kwkktpud.

Conclusion

1 "From George Washington to the Hebrew Congregations of Philadelphia, New York, Charleston, and Richmond, 13 December 1790," *Founders Online*, National Archives, accessed February 14, 2023, https://tinyurl.com/mvu7jpn2. Original source: *The Papers of George Washington*, Presidential Series, vol. 7, *1 December 1790–21 March 1791*, ed. Jack D. Warren Jr. (Charlottesville: University Press of Virginia, 1998), 61–64.

2 "From George Washington to the Hebrew Congregations of Philadelphia, New York, Charleston, and Richmond, 13 December 1790."

3 From Mark Noll interview with Liz Covart, *Ben Franklin's World* podcast, episode 073, "Mark Noll, The Bible in Early America."

4 Robert Middlekauff, *The Glorious Cause: The American Revolution, 1763–1789*, rev. and exp. ed. (Oxford and New York: Oxford

University Press, 2005), 52, 62, 622. Middlekauff was merely artic-
ulating a consensus that has held among American historians now
for over fifty years. Bernard Bailyn and Gordon Wood were among
the first to articulate this view. In his 1967 book, Bailyn described
the *Ideological Origins of the American Revolution* as a "surprising
mix" of "Enlightenment abstractions, and common law precedents,
covenant theology and classical analogy" and—most importantly,
in his view—a "peculiar strain of anti-authoritarianism bred in the
upheaval of the English Civil War." Bailyn, *The Ideological Origins
of the American Revolution*, v–x. Two years later, Wood observed
that the revolutionaries saw the "mandates of covenantal theology"
as complementing, not contradicting, "knowledge about society
reached through the use of history and reason." Referencing the work
of Josiah Quincy II, a graduate of Harvard in the class of 1763, Wood
observed: "It seemed indeed to be a peculiar moment in history
when all knowledge coincided, when classical antiquity, Christian
theology, English empiricism, and European rationalism could all
be linked. Thus Josiah Quincy, like other Americans, could without
any sense of incongruity cite Rousseau, Plutarch, Blackstone, and a
seventeenth-century Puritan all on the same page." Gordon Wood,
The Creation of the American Republic (Chapel Hill: University of
North Carolina Press, 1969), 7. More recent generations of historians
have sought to flesh all this out. And as this ideology began to bridge
gaps between the colonies' elites, so, too, did new moral philosophies
that were giving birth to new expressions of the inner life, using categories like "sensibility" and "passion" and "spirit."

5   Elizabeth Dias, "The Far-Right Christian Quest for Power," *New
York Times*, July 13, 2022, https://tinyurl.com/6fjjk6ad.

Bibliography

Addison, Joseph. *Cato. A tragedy, by Mr. Addison [Seven lines from Seneca].* Boston: printed by Mein and Fleming, and sold by J. Mein at the London Book Store, north side of King-Street, 1767.

Allen, James. *The Poem Which The Committee . . .* Boston: E. Russell, 1772.

Anonymous. *The New-England primer improved. For the more easy attaining the true reading of English. To which is added, the Assembly of Divines catechism.* Boston: 1750.

———. *The Spirit of the Martyrs Revived in the Doctrines of the Reverend George Whitefield, and the Judicious, and Faithful Methodists.* London: T. Cooper, 1740.

Bailyn, Bernard. *The Ideological Origins of the American Revolution.* Cambridge, MA: Belknap Press of Harvard University Press, 1967.

———. *Voyagers to the West.* New York: Knopf, 1986.

Ball, Edward. *Slaves in the Family.* New York: Farrar, Straus & Giroux, 1998.

Balmer, Randall. *Bad Faith: Race and the Rise of the Religious Right.* Grand Rapids, MI: Eerdmans, 2021.

Batwell, Daniel. *A Sermon Preached at York-Town.* Philadelphia: Dunlap, 1775.

Baxter, Richard. *A call to the unconverted, to turn and live.* Boston: Kneeland and Green, 1731.

Bird, Samuel. *The Importance of the Divine Presence*. New Haven, CT: James Parker, 1759.

Blight, David W. *Race and Reunion: The Civil War in American Memory*. Cambridge, MA: Harvard University Press, 2001.

Boyarin, Daniel. *Dying for God: Martyrdom and the Making of Christianity and Judaism*. Palo Alto: Stanford University Press, 1999.

Brown, Christopher Boyd. *Singing the Gospel: Lutheran Hymns and the Success of the Reformation*. Harvard Historical Studies 148. Cambridge, MA: Harvard University Press, 2005.

Bunyan, John. *The Pilgrim's Progress from this World to that which is to Come*. London: printed for Robert Ponder, 1693.

Butler, Jon. *Awash in a Sea of Faith: Christianizing the American People*. Cambridge, MA: Harvard University Press, 1990.

Byrd, James P. *Sacred Scripture, Sacred War: The Bible and the American Revolution*. New York: Oxford University Press, 2013.

Calvert, Jane E. *Quaker Constitutionalism and the Political Thought of John Dickinson*. New York: Cambridge University Press, 2009.

Carretta, Vincent. *Equiano the African: Biography of a Self-Made Man*. Athens: University of Georgia Press, 2005.

Castelli, Elizabeth A. *Martyrdom and Memory: Early Christian Culture Making*. New York: Columbia University Press, 2004.

Church, Benjamin. *The Times: A Poem*. Boston: Thomas Fleet, 1765.

Cressy, David. *Bonfires and Bells: National Memory and the Protestant Calendar in Elizabethan and Stuart England*. Berkeley: University of California Press, 1989.

Cronon, William. *Changes in the Land: Indians, Colonists, and the Ecology of New England*. New York: Hill & Wang, 1983.

Cushing, Harry Alonzo, ed. *The Writings of Samuel Adams: vol. 1, 1764–1769*. New York: G. P. Putnam's Sons, 1904.

Danforth, Samuel. *A Brief Recognition of New England's Errand into the Wilderness*. Cambridge, MA: Samuel Green, 1671.

Dargan, William T. *Lining Out the Word: Dr. Watts Hymn Singing in the Music of Black Americans*. Berkeley: University of California Press, 2006.

Davies, Samuel. *The curse of cowardice. A sermon preached to the militia of Hanover County, in Virginia, at a general muster, May 8, 1758. With a view to raise a company for Captain Samuel Meredith. By Samuel Davies, A.M.* London: printed. Boston: re-printed and sold by Z. Fowle and S. Draper, opposite the Lion & Bell, in Marlborough-Street, 1759; Woodbridge, NJ: re-printed and sold by James Parker, 1759; New-York: re-printed and sold by Samuel Parker, at the New-Printing Office in Beaver-Street, 1759.

———. "On the Defeat of General Braddock, Going to Forte-De-Quesne." In *Sermons on Important Subjects, by the Late Reverend and Pious Samuel Davies, A.M. Some Time President of the College in New Jersey.* Boston: Lincoln & Edmands, 1810.

———. *The Duty of Christians to Propagate their Religion among Heathens: Earnestly Recommended to the Masters of Negroe Slaves in Virginia. A Sermon preached in Hanover January 8, 1757.* London: printed by J. Oliver in Bartholomew-Close, 1758.

———. *Religion and Public Spirit.* Portsmouth, NH: Daniel Fowle, 1762.

Delehaye, Hippolyte. *Les passions des martyrs et les genres littéraires,* 2nd ed. Brussels: Société des Bollandistes, 1966.

Demos, John. *The Unredeemed Captive.* New York: Random House, 1995.

Du Mez, Kristin Kobes. *Jesus and John Wayne: How White Evangelicals Corrupted a Faith and Fractured a Nation.* New York: Liveright Publishing, 2020.

Dunn, R. S. *Sugar and Slaves: The Rise of the Planter Class in the English West Indies, 1624–1713.* Chapel Hill: University of North Carolina Press, 2000.

Dyer, Justin. "Is America a Christian Nation? Yes and No." *Washington Post,* January 3, 2023.

Eastburn, Robert. *A faithful narrative, of the many dangers and sufferings, as well as wonderful and surprizing deliverances of Robert Eastburn, during his late captivity among the Indians: together with some remarks upon the country of Canada, and* the religion and policy of its inhabitants; the whole intermixed with devout reflections. By Robert Eastburn. Published at the earnest request of many persons, for the benefit of the public. With a recommendatory preface, by the Rev. Gilbert Tennent. [Six lines from Psalms]. Philadelphia: printed by William Dunlap, 1758.

Elliott, J. H. The Old World and the New, 1492–1650, Canto ed. New York: Cambridge University Press, 1970.

Fanestil, John. Mrs. Hunter's Happy Death: Lessons on Living from People Preparing to Die. New York: Doubleday, 2006.

———. "The Print Practice of Martyrology in British North America, 1688–1787." PhD diss., University of Southern California, 2017.

Flavel, John. The Mystery of Providence. West Linn, OR: Monergism Books, 2018.

Franklin, Benjamin. The Causes of the Present Distractions in America. New York: F.B., 1774.

———. Observations concerning the Increase of Mankind, Peopling of Countries,&c. Boston: printed and sold by S. Kneeland in Queen-Street, 1755.

———. (Richard Saunders pseudonym). Poor Richard, 1733, An Almanack for the Year of Christ 1733. Philadelphia: Benjamin Franklin, 1733.

Gatti, Hilary, ed. Essays on Giordano Bruno. Princeton, NJ: Princeton University Press, 2011.

Gershberg, Zac, and Sean Illing. The Paradox of Democracy: Free Speech, Open Media, and Perilous Persuasion. Chicago: University of Chicago Press, 2022.

Goodman, Glenda. "'The Tears I Shed at the Songs of Thy Church': Seventeenth-Century Musical Piety in the English Atlantic World." Journal of the American Musicological Society 65, no. 3 (2012): 691–725.

Gordon-Reed, Annette. The Hemingses of Monticello. New York: W. W. Norton, 2008.

Gorski, Philip S. American Babylon: Christianity and Democracy before and after Trump. London and New York: Routledge, 2020.

Gorski, Philip S., and Samuel L. Perry. *The Flag and the Cross: White Christian Nationalism and the Threat to American Democracy*. New York: Oxford University Press, 2022.

Grasso, Christopher. *A Speaking Aristocracy: Transforming Public Discourse in Eighteenth-Century Connecticut*. Williamsburg: Omohundro Institute of Early American History & Culture.

Griffith, R. Marie. *Moral Combat: How Sex Divided American Christians and Fractured American Politics*. New York: Basic Books, 2017.

Hakluyt, Richard. *The Principal Navigations, Voyages, Traffiques and Discoveries of the English Nation*. London: 1589.

Hall, David D. *Cultures of Print: Essays in the History of the Book*. Amherst: University of Massachusetts Press, 1996.

Hancock, John. *An oration; delivered March 5, 1774, at the request of the inhabitants of the town of Boston: to commemorate the bloody tragedy of the fifth of March 1770. By the Honorable John Hancock, Esq; [Five lines in Latin from Virgil]*. Boston: printed by Eddes and Gill, in Queen Street, 1774.

Hannah-Jones, Nikole. *The 1619 Project: A New Origin Story*. New York: One World, 2021.

Hinderaker, Eric. *Boston's Massacre*. Cambridge, MA: Harvard University Press, 2017.

Hoffer, Peter Charles. *When Benjamin Franklin Met the Reverend Whitefield: Enlightenment, Revival, and the Power of the Printed Word*. Baltimore: John Hopkins University Press, 2013.

Holton, Woody. *Liberty Is Sweet: The Hidden History of the American Revolution*. New York: Simon & Schuster, 2021.

Humphrey, Carol Sue. *The American Revolution and the Press: The Promise of Independence*. Evanston, IL: Medill School of Journalism/Northwestern University Press, 2013.

Isaacson, Walter. *A Benjamin Franklin Reader*. New York: Simon & Schuster, 2005.

Janes, Dominic, and Alex Houen. *Martyrdom and Terrorism: Pre-Modern to Contemporary Perspectives*. New York: Oxford University Press, 2014.

Jewell, William. *The Golden Cabinet of True Treasure*. London: John Crosley, 1612.

Jones, Robert P. *White Too Long: The Legacy of White Supremacy in American Christianity*. New York: Simon & Schuster, 2020.

Joyce, William Leonard, ed. *Printing and Society in Early America*. Worcester, MA: American Antiquarian Society, 1983.

Kendi, Ibram X. *Stamped from the Beginning: The Definitive History of Racist Ideas in America*. New York: Perseus Books, 2016.

Kidd, Thomas S. *God of Liberty: A Religious History of the American Revolution*. New York: Basic Books, 2010.

King, John N. *Foxe's Book of Martyrs and Early Modern Print Culture*. Cambridge: Cambridge University Press, 2006.

Kobre, Sidney. "The Revolutionary Colonial Press—A Social Interpretation." *Journalism Quarterly* 20 (1943): 193–204.

Leonard, Abiel. *A prayer, composed for the benefit of the soldiery, in the American army, to assist them in their private devotions; and recommended to their particular use. By Abiel Leonard, A.M. Chaplain to General Putnam's regiment, in said army*. Cambridge, MA: printed and sold by S. & E. Hall, 1775.

Locke, John. *Two Treatises of Government*. London: A. Millar, 1764.

Lum, Kathryn Gin. *Heathen: Religion and Race in American History*. Cambridge, MA: Harvard University Press, 2022.

Lyons, Jonathan. *The Society for Useful Knowledge: How Benjamin Franklin and Friends Brought the Enlightenment to America*. New York: Bloomsbury Press, 2013.

MacDonald, Ruth K. *Christian's Children: The Influence of John Bunyan's The Pilgrim's Progress on American Children's Literature*. New York: Peter Lang, 1989.

Mancall, Peter. *Hakluyt's Promise: An Elizabethan's Obsession for English America*. New Haven, CT: Yale University Press, 2007.

Mason, Laura. *Singing the French Revolution: Popular Culture and Politics, 1787–1799*. Ithaca, NY: Cornell University Press, 1996.

Mather, Cotton. *Just Commemorations: The Death of Good Men, Considered*. Boston: Bartholomew Green, 1715.

McBride, Spencer. *Pulpit & Nation: Clergymen and the Politics of Revolutionary America*. Charlottesville: University of Virginia Press, 2016.

McKenna, George. *The Puritan Origins of American Patriotism*. New Haven, CT: Yale University Press, 2007.

Middlekauff, Robert. *The Glorious Cause: The American Revolution, 1763–1789*, rev. and exp. ed. Oxford and New York: Oxford University Press, 2005.

Miller, John C. *John Adams: Pioneer in Propaganda*. Boston: Little, Brown, 1936.

Misencik, Paul R. *The Original American Spies: Seven Covert Agents of the Revolutionary War*. Jefferson, NC: McFarland, 2014.

Morgan, Edmund S. *American Slavery, American Freedom: The Ordeal of Colonial Virginia*. New York: Norton, 1995, 1975.

Moss, Candida. *Ancient Christian Martyrdom: Diverse Practices, Theologies, and Traditions*. New Haven, CT: Yale University Press, 2012.

Mueller, Justin C. "America's Herrenvolk Democracy Is a Social Democracy for the White Majority." *Milwaukee Independent*, November 3, 2017.

Musurillo, Herbert. *The Acts of the Christian Martyrs*. Oxford: Clarendon Press, 1972.

Nash, Gary B. *First City: Philadelphia and the Forging of Historical Memory*. Philadelphia: University of Pennsylvania Press, 2002.

Noll, Mark A. *In the Beginning Was the Word: The Bible in American Public Life, 1492–1783*. Oxford: Oxford University Press, 2016.

Onishi, Bradley. *Preparing for War: The Extremist History of White Christian Nationalism—and What Comes Next*. Minneapolis: Broadleaf Books, 2023.

Paine, Thomas. *Common Sense; Addressed to the Inhabitants of America On the following interesting Subjects . . . The Third Edition*. Philadelphia: R. Bell, 1776.

Parkinson, Robert G. *The Common Cause: Creating Race and Nation in the American Revolution*. Chapel Hill: University of North Carolina Press, 2016.

Phillips, Christopher. "Cotton Mather Brings Isaac Watt's Hymns to America; or How to Perform a Hymn without Singing It." *The New England Quarterly* 85, no. 2 (2012): 203.

Purcell, Sarah J. *Sealed with Blood: War, Sacrifice, and Memory in Revolutionary America*. Philadelphia: University of Pennsylvania Press, 2003.

Raboteau, Albert J. *Slave Religion: The "Invisible Institution" in the Antebellum South*. New York: Oxford University Press, 1978.

Rath, Richard Cullen. *How Early America Sounded*. Ithaca, NY: Cornell University Press, 2003.

Roney, Jessica Choppin. *Governed by a Spirit of Opposition: The Origins of American Political Practice in Colonial Philadelphia*. Baltimore: Johns Hopkins University Press, 2014.

Routley, Erik. *Christian Hymns Observed: When in Our Music God Is Glorified*. Princeton, NJ: Prestige Publications, 1982.

Salisbury, Neal, ed. *The Sovereignty and Goodness of God, by Mary Rowlandson, with Related Documents*. Boston and New York: Bedford/St. Martin's, 1997.

Schlesinger, Arthur M. "A Note on Songs as Patriot Propaganda 1765–1776." *The William and Mary Quarterly* 11, no. 1 (1954): 78–88.

Seymour, George Dudley. *Documentary Life of Nathan Hale: Comprising all Available Official and Private Documents Bearing on the Life of the Patriot, Together with an Appendix, Showing the Background of His Life . . .* New-Haven: priv. printed for the author, 1941.

Shaffer, Jason. "Making 'an Excellent Die': Death, Mourning, and Patriotism in the Propaganda Plays of the American Revolution." *Early American Literature* 41, no. 1 (2006): 1–27.

Shy, John W. *A People Numerous and Armed: Reflections on the Military Struggle for American Independence*. Ann Arbor: University of Michigan Press, 1990.

Silver, Peter. *Our Savage Neighbors: How Indian War Transformed Early America*. New York: W. W. Norton, 2008.

Stillman, Samuel. *Death, the last enemy, destroyed by Christ*. Philadelphia: Joseph Crukshank, 1776.

Stout, Harry S. *The Divine Dramatist: George Whitefield and the Rise of Modern Evangelicalism*. Grand Rapids, MI: William B. Eerdmans, 1991.

Taves, Ann. *Fits, Trances, & Visions: Experiencing Religion and Explaining Experience from Wesley to James*. Princeton, NJ: Princeton University Press, 1999.

Taylor, Jeremy. *Antiquitates christianae, or, The history of the life and death of the holy Jesus as also the lives acts and martyrdoms of his Apostles: in two parts*. London: printed by R. Norton for R. Royston, 1675.

_____. *The great exemplar of sanctity and holy life according to the Christian institution described in the history of the life and death of the ever blessed Jesus Christ the saviour of the world: with considerations and discourses upon the several parts of the story and prayers fitted to the several mysteries: in three parts*. London: printed by R.N. for Francis Ash, 1649.

_____. *The rule and exercises of holy living. In which are described the means and instruments of obtaining every vertue, and the remedies against every vice, and considerations serving to the resisting all temptations. Together with prayers containing the whole duty of a Christian, and the parts of devotion fitted to all occasions, and furnish'd for all necessities*. London: printed [by R. Norton] for Richard Royston, 1650.

Tennent, Gilbert. *The danger of an unconverted ministry, considered in a sermon on Mark VI. 34. Preached at Nottingham, in Pennsylvania, March 8. anno 1739,40. By Gilbert Tennent, A.M. and Minister of the Gospel in New-Brunswick, New-Jersey [Five lines from Jeremiah]*. Philadelphia: printed by Benjamin Franklin, in Market-Street, 1740.

Thornton, John. *Africa and Africans in the Making of the Atlantic World, 1400–1800*, 2nd ed. New York: Cambridge University Press, 1998.

Tisby, Jemar. *The Color of Compromise: The Truth about the American Church's Complicity in Racism*. Grand Rapids, MI: Zondervan, 2017.

Tolles, Frederick B. *Quakers and the Atlantic Culture*. New York: Octagon Books, 1960.

Tomlin, T. J. "Astrology's from Heaven Not from Hell." *Early American Studies* 8, no. 2 (Spring 2010): 288–321.

van den Berghe, Pierre L. *Race and Racism: A Comparative Perspective*. New York: Wiley, 1967.

Watts, Isaac. *Divine Songs Attempted in Easy Language for the Use of Children . . . Seventh Edition*. Boston: Kneeland & Green for Henchman, 1730.

———. *Hymns and Spiritual Songs*. Boston: ?, 1720?

———. *Hymns and Spiritual Songs in Three Books . . . The Thirty Third Edition*. London: Longman and Ware, 1771.

Weimer, Adrian Chastain. *Martyrs' Mirror: Persecution and Holiness in Early New England*. New York: Oxford University Press, 2011.

Whitehead, Andrew, and Samuel Perry. *Taking America Back for God: Christian Nationalism in the United States*. New York: Oxford University Press, 2020.

Wood, Gordon. *The Creation of the American Republic*. Chapel Hill: University of North Carolina Press, 1969.

Wroth, Lawrence C. *The Colonial Printer*. New York: Dover, 1994.

Index